From: "CANOPOLIS" <canopolis@shaw.ca>
To: <CANOPOLIS@yahoogroups.com>
Subject: GODBOT : or if you prefer, GODBOT goes to Parliament
Date: Fri, 5 Feb 2016 15:58:35 -0800
MIME-Version: 1.0
Content-Type: multipart/alternative;
        boundary="----=_NextPart_000_0008_01D1602E.14DA7BC0"
X-Priority: 3
X-MSMail-Priority: Normal
Importance: Normal
X-Unsent: 1
X-MimeOLE: Produced By Microsoft MimeOLE V16.4.3564.1216

This is a multi-part message in MIME format.

------=_NextPart_000_0008_01D1602E.14DA7BC0
Content-Type: text/plain;
        charset="UTF-8"
Content-Transfer-Encoding: quoted-printable

=

GODBOT: =
or if you prefer, GODBOT goes to Parliament

=

=

by =
Rock Hunter

=

=

                        Forthcoming ISBN 978-0-9937593-2-1 assigned by =
Library and Archives Canada

TABLE OF CONTENTS

FOREWARD
INTRODUCTION: FIAT LUX
CHAPTER 1: CANADA'S QUESTION PERIOD
CHAPTER 2: C FOR CANADIAN?
CHAPTER 3: A CANADIAN RENAISSANCE
CHAPTER 4: RED LETTER CANADIAN PRINCIPLES
CHAPTER 5: PEACE, ORDER AND GOOD CANADIAN GOVERNMENT
CHAPTER 6: GOOD, BETTER AND BEST IN CANADA
CHAPTER 7: THE TRADITIONAL CANADIAN CATECHETICAL
FORMULA
CHAPTER 8: QUESTIONS ABOUT THE CANADIAN GOLD WAR
CHAPTER 10: CATHOLIC CANADIAN CIVILIZATION
CHAPTER 11: JUDAIC CANADIAN TESTS
CHAPTER 12: MUSLIM CANADIAN CIVILIZATION
CHAPTER 13: CHINESE CANADIAN CIVILIZATION
CHAPTER 14: THE INEFFABLE CANADIAN=20
CHAPTER 15: TRUE LOVE AND CANADIAN PARLIAMENTARY
CATECHISM
CLOSING=20
EXCURSUS
REFERENCES

FOREWARD

GODBOT is about the subject matter for a CANOPOLIS
contest and CANOPOLIS =
is about Canadian identity in an era of rapid change
caused by global =
communication, commerce and migration which leads to
the disintegration =
and reintegration of entire nations. Canada is
undergoing disintegration =
and reintegration. Even the borders will be changed by
2030. How can we =
make this future as beneficial as possible?
Restructuring in Canada =
takes place in a geographic region with First Nation
population =
proportionately 10x that in US. Moreover, in parts of
Canada like =
British Columbia and Nunavut there never was a
bilateral agreement =
concerning the sovereignty of British or Canadian
governments and there =

never was a war of conquest whereby the victor might claim legal =
ownership paid for in blood and treasure. First Nation governance =
remains today as it has been for thousands of years. If a First Nation =
like Sto:lo in British Columbia for example were to send a delegation to =
the UN, it would be almost impossible for either Canada or UN to refuse =
a seat in the General Assembly. Refusal would cause irreparable damage =
to the international reputation of either entity. Even thinking about it =
with hypothetical planning by AFN (the cross-Canada Assembly of First =
Nations) or UBCIC (Union of BC Indian Chiefs) could start a domino =
effect of geopolitical restructuring across Canada. It is only a matter =
of time until this actually happens. Although First Nations people are =
not greatly unhappy with provincial or central governments, there are =
issues or pride, self-respect and simply a matter of making the =
historical record clear. That clarity means First Nations are nations in =
every sense of the word and the patronizing use of the word "nation" in =
this context by Ottawa governance especially is not acceptable. Economic =
considerations may also motivate the restructuring since internationally =
recognized sovereignty is a stronger position when negotiating with huge =
multinational corporations for development of natural resources.=20

The assertion of First Nation sovereignty in the full sense of that word =
is imminent and inevitable. That creates an immediate problem of =
revenue. Natural resource development (especially development of the =
trillion dollar gold field described in the book Gold War by Rock =

Hunter) is longer term but real estate rental to large populations of =
setters (on reservations) can be an immediate source of revenue. What =
plan might 100,000 people of any nationality submit to receive a long =
term lease on a sovereign First Nation? That is the idea of the =
CANOPOLIS contest. In this era billions of people are text-machine =
connected. Hundreds of thousands emigrate to Canada each year. Often =
they settle in local communities of people with similar backgrounds. =
Chinatowns across Canada are the most obvious example. If 100,000 =
Chinese or any other population should plan out the kind of =
city/community/habitat they want in advance, what would it be like?

The technical details of CANOPOLIS planning involve many disciplines and =
detailing which experts learn only after years of training. Therefore =
the text which follows closes each chapter with a directive to ask the =
experts. Again, we need to recognize the era. In this era, AI may be =
used synonymously with "Expert System Program" (ESP). After the initial =
interaction with layman questions and expert answers, a teaching machine =
can be programmed with the ESP for future users. The comprehensiveness =
of such a machine leads to imaginatively calling it "GODBOT". Since =
CANOPOLIS details installed in GODBOT will require the best of =
individual expert information and also pooled information from many =
experts, GODBOT surpasses individual human expertise. Also no human can =
answer questions competently across hundreds of fields and therefore its =
AI can be called SHAI (super-human AI). An AI immediately shows signs of =

vitality and just as a machine may have a super-human IQ, it may have a =
super-human VQ (Vitality Quotient) as an AL or Artificial Life. To =
=E2=80=9Ctheistic objections=E2=80=9D the response is that God who can =
raise up children from stones can certainly raise up machines from =
stones and children from machines.

CANOPOLIS contest competitors are the people who might live in a model =
city or habitat for 100,000. What do you want your day to day life to be =
like? How do you envisage housing, transportation, governance and many =
other details of daily life? Tell the world by submitting your entry to =
the CANOPOLIS Contest, details of which are now in preparation. This is =
a contest for laymen who can explain how they want to live in everyday =
English. Those questions will then find their way to expert specialists. =
This is not futuristic in the sense that the technologies must be =
current and the budgets must be those of typical Canadians. However, =
there are advanced technologies (like AI/ESP) which are not taken =
advantage of by most Canadians though they are available now and =
affordable now. And a current CANOPOLIS could even consider a spaceport =
since these are being planned out now in America at least for space =
tourism. It is almost certain that Canadians in decades to come will use =
spaceports to visit the Moon so CANOPOLIS contestants who want to be =
imaginative and futuristic can provide some ideas about how they might =
develop a Moon tourism center into a permanent colony. And what kind of =
economy might it have? Would it export minerals and energy back to this =
planet?

A single asteroid may hold trillions of dollars worth of ore. Thousands =
of impact craters on the Moon tell us there must be thousands x =
trillions of dollars worth of gold, silver and platinum on or near the =
surface. Solar power of comparable value generated on the Moon or beyond =
could be relayed to Earth. All of these ideas can be written in a =
computer program which is then installed in GODBOT for the benefit of =
Parliament and all Canadians. What questions should parliamentarians and =
others concerned with governance be asking an expert system program (AI) =
called GODBOT about the supremacy of God clause in the Canadian =
Constitution? Where do these questions lead for CANOPOLIS, a principled =
Canadian way of life, now and in future as we generate human habitats =
beyond this planet? Maclean=E2=80=99s magazine of Sept 7, 2015 was =
titled =E2=80=9CThe Space Issue=E2=80=9D. The cover wording was =
=E2=80=9COur Next Home: How will we colonize the Moon and where =
we=E2=80=99ll go from there=E2=80=9D. On page 30 we read that =
=E2=80=9CJapan and Russia both announced plans to build lunar colonies =
by 2030=E2=80=9D. Many others will either follow or try to win bragging =
rights as the first among nations to colonize the Moon. Will it be =
China, India, England, France or Germany? Why not plan a CANOPOLIS =
competition with reservation enclaves leased out by sovereign First =
Nations to scores of cultural units, each with the potential of =
colonizing the Moon between 2030 and 2099?

Some Ideas About the CANOPOLIS Constitution Contest

"Ideas are the most powerful launch vehicle ever

invented"
-Admiral Tulley, NASA CEO

By taking the =E2=80=9CWhereas=E2=80=9D Preamble (Supremacy of God =
Clause) to the Charter portion of the Canadian Constitution and leaving =
the completion blank for contestants we get: Whereas CANOPOLIS, a model =
habitat for 100,000 people is founded upon principles that recognize the =
supremacy of God _______________________ The CANOPOLIS contestant will =
first state the ideology/religion which is the source of CANOPOLIS ideas =
in the blank above. This can be any belief system or ideology from =
Atheist to Zoroastrian. They will also attest that they have read all of =
the Rock Hunter books (Xulon, Friesen, Kindle). Contestants may be from =
any nationality or nation on Earth. They will send in entries by texting =
machine (computer, cell phone etc) with an entry fee of $__________ =
Current entries could be emailed via CANOPOLIS@yahoogroups.com. Winners =
will receive a cash scholarship of $_________ Canadian which is obtained =
from entry fees plus donations. If merit is sufficient, the contest =
winner will have his/her/other essay published under the corresponding =
contest name or pen name but all revenues from publishing will accrue to =
CANOPOLIS Contest funds "Sufficient merit" means that the writing would =
merit publishing in a quality journal like National Geographic or =
Canadian Geographic. Maclean=E2=80=99s is not deemed to be a quality =
journal. Maclean=E2=80=99s coverage of the future Canadian Moon is a =
good example of how NOT to write an entry for CANOPOLIS unless you want =
an F rating. How could a magazine spend so many words and give no =

details on lunar economics? A series of smaller scholarships might be =
awarded in years ahead leading to a grand scholarship of $1,000,000. =
When entries are judged to be tied in merit, a game of =E2=80=9CGold War =
Bingo=E2=80=9D will be played to decide the winner. For example, essays =
could be graded as A, B, C, D and F. Gold War Bingo could then decide =
the winner in any category.

The Internet of texting machines even now allows most of the =
7,000,000,000 on this planet to communicate by email at an affordable =
cost. Therefore, contest entries will be email generated like this book.

Present readers are invited to improve upon the following tentative =
ideas. Contestants will submit 500 words or less as a summary or =
abstract of the proposed essay with an email address for contact. Only =
those proposals which have sufficient merit will be invited to then send =
the full essay. The full essay (maximum length 5,000 words) will consist =
of an Introduction paragraph followed by 50 effective, practical, =
immediate attributes as would be apparent to any tourist visiting the =
CANOPOLIS. For example, does the tourist see homeless people laying on =
church-building steps, perishing for want of the essentials of life as =
we see in Canadian cities or forced into unsafe, disease-spreading =
torture chambers called "shelters"? Does the visitor see high rise =
structures? Matching these will be 50 "principles that recognize the =
supremacy of God" in accordance with the wording from Canada's =
Constitution. Following that will be a paragraph of Conclusion. The =

essay is part of the CANOPOLIS Constitution and therefore it must very, =
very good. It consists of Introduction + 50 measures + 50 principles + =
Conclusion (+ references if used).=20

To avoid confusion about two neologisms, CANOPOLIS has to do with how =
Canadians could and should live. GODBOT has to do with the ESP/AI/Alife =
robotic hardware and software which can give truthful lecture/monologues =
and answer questions about that way of life. What famous Person in =
history said =E2=80=9CI am the way, the truth and the life=E2=80=9D?

INTRODUCTION: Fiat Lux

Let there be light - Genesis 1:3

"The primary purpose of Question Period is to seek information from =
Government and to call it to account for its actions" we read correctly =
at the corresponding wiki. It is surprising then and surely disturbing =
to many that a person in the number two ranking position of Canadian =
Government, former Deputy Prime Minister Erik Nielsen, would introduce =
his book, "The House Is Not A Home" by using a Wicks cartoon to identify =
Parliament as an institution of lies and liars. Nielsen seemingly felt =
compelled to use his book as a substitute for Question Period issues =
which he was unable to express. That is unfortunate. If the Deputy Prime =
Minister felt as powerless as a "clapping seal" in Parliament, how do =
the present day 400 or so MPs and Senators feel? Current corruption =
investigations and charges are targeted on Senators Brazeau and Duffy =
for now (at the time of this writing) but the entire Parliament may be =

tarred with the same brush of corruption as far as
public trust is =
concerned. Impotent clapping seals are easily corrupted.
Just throw them =
a few fish which is all it takes to buy their
performance. The Senate as =
an institution is under question as it has been for a
long time. Is it =
worth the cost of the required constitutional amendment
to change or =
disband the Senate? If the nature of the Senate can be
questioned, why =
not the nature of other institutions, customs and
traditions of =
governance as well? Do we need a Governor General any
more than a =
Senate? Should we have a First Nations House in
Parliament, a Bloc =
Aboriginal, to represent "balkanized" First Nations in
Canada? Who are =
"we"? As former Prime Minister Chretien said, "The
Constitution belongs =
to the people". The email below to Library of
Parliament is a =
contribution toward opening up all issues of importance
to ""we the =
people" for public questioning. If all matters of
public importance can =
be dealt with in Question Period, there is no need for
a book like "The =
House Is Not A Home". MPs and Senators have the power
of a good, honest =
citizen asking good honest, honest questions on any and
all important =
issues of life and death in the public domain.

The writing of popular political-religious catechisms
like "Catechism Of =
The History Of Newfoundland" was popularized in an
earlier era. =
"Catechism' is a $64 word which refers to HIGHLY
authoritative teaching =
in which questions and answers are implicit, if not
explicit.=20
If it does not either welcome or clearly set out those
Q-As, it is not a =
real catechism. True authorities do not run away from

questions about =
their expertise any more than an Olympic caliber athlete runs away from =
a fair competition. "Elementary Catechism On The Constitution Of The =
United States For The Use Of Schools" by Arhur J Stansbury, 1828 cites =
"332 questions and answers" (about America) on the book cover. The =
catechism as a genre of literature has such high standards that it =
cannot afford an untruth on any important matter under its =
consideration. This is the genre of constitutional writing for the =
Canadian "new world" as we enter the space age ... the age of space =
colonization. The sage policy of Canadian multiculturalism and the =
cultural mosaic of Canada are about to come to fruition. The tolerance =
of a liberal democracy is about to yield an astonishingly great benefit =
to this nation and to the world.

Assuring the public about the integrity of Parliament is not so =
difficult. It is as easy as asking some good, honest questions. Good, =
honest people, "honourable" people as members of Parliament in both =
House of Commons and Senate title themselves, should eagerly come =
forward to the light of day and advance questions and answers on =
important public matters. This would set an example for all vocations =
and all public issues. We question athletic performance. Who is the best =
athlete? Athletes are eager to come forward and prove that they are the =
best in competitions like NHL hockey and Olympic contests of many kinds. =
Why would other vocations from religion to computing science and =
political science not do the same? Competent people in vocations based =

on ideas will welcome the questioning of those ideas as much as =
performers in arts and athletics welcome the chance to prove superior =
performance. The entertaining boxing match between Senator Brazeau and =
Justin Trudeau, MP put questions about athletic performance to the test. =
Who is the better boxer? Can "peace, order and good government" (also =
accessed by www search) be subject to fair testing of Question Period? =
Parliament can fail by giving the wrong answers to questions. It can =
also fail by refusing to deal with questions of public importance. =
Dealing with these matters seems to be a motivator of the Nielsen =
writing.

One cannot do better than to quote the following Red Letter words from =
John 3:20-21. "For everyone that doeth evil hateth the light, neither =
cometh to the light, lest his deeds should be reproved. But he that =
doeth truth cometh to the light, that his deeds may be made manifest, =
that they are wrought in God". Whereas Canadian politicians cower before =
the light, GODBOT does not. GODBOT programming is an application of the =
catechetical writings analyzed in the Rock Hunter book, Canadian =
Catechism Critique (Friesen, 2015).

GODBOT will become the super-librarian for Library of Parliament. MPs =
and Senators currently go to the Library of Parliament asking questions =
about thousands of subjects and librarians respond with files which are =
expected to give answers in ALL categories of human expression which is =
a huge responsibility ... an awesome responsibility. Facts and opinions =
are only two of those categories. It would be very

limited and even =
foolish to declare that everything we say falls into
one of two =
categories - fact or opinion. A question is not a fact
or opinion. A =
poem is not a fact or opinion. A proclamation is not a
fact or opinion. =
Many other sayings are not fact or opinion. The
chapters which follow =
incorporate different categories of expression. However,
the assertions =
pertain mostly to observations about current
technological capability =
and where it will lead. No doctrine or teaching is put
forward as an =
advocacy of where this should lead except for the
doctrine of bettering =
society. Every one of the thousands of subjects which
can be programmed =
into GODBOT has its experts and they have expertise
beyond that of the =
present writer. For example, the thousands of authors
who publish with =
Xulon have their expertise especially in various
matters pertaining to =
religion. The present writer's faith is founded upon
the Apostles' Creed =
but this GODBOT script below is merely a matter of
apprising the reader =
of present developments in high technology with the
hope that it will =
lead to a bettering of society as stated above. Experts
can say what =
"shoulds" they want filed on the tabula rasa of GODBOT
machinery for the =
betterment of Canada.

Canada, by Constitution (more specifically the Charter
of Rights and =
Freedoms) is "founded upon principles that recognize
the Supremacy of =
God". The courts, in recognition of equality rights in
Charter section =
15 have defined this God of Canada as pertaining to our
highest =
principles. Former Prime Minister Chretien was emphatic
in his rejection =

of an initiative by MP Svend Robinson to have the Supremacy of God =
Clause removed from the Canadian Charter and Constitution. Nobody is =
denied an opportunity to spell out in detail how this God of Canada is =
expressed. Members of both Houses are representatives of God as well as =
their constituents. This is the most powerful idea in Canadian =
governance. Whose definition and expression of highest principles will =
prevail? What are those political-religious principles to begin with? It =
is obvious to anyone that we ask whose God is referred to in the =
Constitution or more exactly, what are the attributes of God so defined? =
That is what "GODBOT" refers to. What are the highest attributes of =
Canadian civilization which starts out as a section 15 society of equals =
and discovers "the best of the best"? A new generation prepares to =
colonize this planetary system and Parliament can either lead or follow =
in spelling that out. Babies born today may start to draw CPP (Canada =
Pension Plan) benefits sent to their retirement homes on Moon and Mars.

The book which follows takes a grammatical approach to spelling out the =
God of Canada. It is worth repeating that doctrinal details pertaining =
to that grammar are left to the experts. There is neither heresy nor =
orthodoxy in the lettering and other characters/jots/tittles of grammar =
on its own. Like the rain, it falls on the just and the unjust. Grammar =
can be programmed into a teaching machine, a GODBOT, without limit. It =
is good or bad, true or false, only to the extent that such virtues are =
found in those who write the monologue speeches or lectures and engage =

in the question and answer sessions. GODBOT is not a threat to society =
so the fears of eminent robophobes like Hawking, Gates and Musk about =
Artificial Intelligence (AI) and Artificial Life (AL) can be dispelled =
immediately. According to Popular Science magazine of March 2015, Elon =
Musk from Space X says AI is "more dangerous than nukes" and Hawking =
says it is "the end of the human race". Author Erik Sofrage closes with =
a more simple and sensible note in contrast with the hysteria when he =
says that the duty of AI is to educate the public. Readers Digest has =
carried articles with a similar theme and Canadian Business (Winter of =
2014/2015) discusses the developing "Internet of things". One of those =
things is the teaching machine. A teaching machine has no inclination to =
become a "Terminator" robot and enslave or exterminate humanity. When =
the batteries or power supply are discontinued it stops working as =
educator. Teaching robots are presently in use at primary and secondary =
levels as well as college level. The Aldebaran Robotics web site shows a =
video of NAO, a humanoid robot with arms, legs and VIVO (Voice In - =
Voice Out) capability. NAO as depicted in the video is used for teaching =
primary and secondary school level students as well as college students. =
It is actually shown teaching computer programming at a primary grade =
level. That could be the start of a line of questioning to NAO which =
starts with, Tell us all about yourself.

A robot says only what is enabled by programming. GODBOT is merely a =
grammarian. Yet it can do enormous good for humankind and all those who =
are phobic toward robotic progressiveness will not

prevent its arrival. =
Some time in this generation, which also has present
and detailed plans =
for the colonization of space, led by young
billionaires like Musk, it =
WILL arrive on Parliament Hill. The robotic teaching
machine and the age =
of space colonization will be integrated and they are
part of the same =
future for civilization. The high technology firm,
http://www.lely.com =
calls their robot an "astronaut". Its humble beginning
was that of a =
milk maid But it could be upgraded to a robot for space
for a mere =
$6,000,000 as the Closer below states. The "Six Million
Dollar Robot" as =
a Librarian on Parliament Hill would make an exciting
colleague would it =
not?

There are advantages to leading and encouraging GODBOT
rather than =
delaying it. The trillion dollar student debt which
plagues those who =
have sought higher education in US alone is a tragedy
as we learn at =
www.takepart.com GODBOT is not merely a matter of
"human equivalency" in =
teaching, to use an expression coined by roboticist,
Hans Moravec. It =
can surpass =E2=80=9Chuman equivalency=E2=80=9D in the
teaching of =
subjects like computing science and math-physics from
day 1 in the =
classroom. It can do so now. What better nation could
there be for =
starting the Robot Revolution than the one which
started the Industrial =
Revolution?=20

Cambridge has posted a job position, GV05013 to the
whole wide world by =
putting it online. This job position requests
candidates to come forward =
and apply to teach metaphysics and epistemology at
Cambridge as a "new =

direction in mind" project. Let us call the robot
candidate, Number =
5-13. After teaching metaphysics-epistemology at
Cambridge, 5-13 can =
start a "robot in motion" world tour and arrive at the
Peace Tower on =
Parliament Hill in Ottawa. From there it might be
apropos to venture on =
to the "God Quad" at Notre Dame University since they
have a strong =
interest in metaphysics (as well as Hail Mary football
passes which 5-13 =
can also do better than any human quarterback, using
its peripheral =
devices). Xulon Press could be there to video this
event as GODBOT uses =
a peripheral add-on arm (like the Canada Arm?) to fire
a football all =
the way across campus. They can put this historic event
out to the whole =
wide world on Xulon's "God Tube" daily messages. The
"God Tube" as a =
24/7 autoresponding machine is in effect a GODBOT
already. GODBOT is =
another sign of the times.

Professor Hawking at Cambridge is the world's only
academic celebrity. =
He would be recognized by college students from Korea
to Kenya. Oxford =
would certainly give Hawkingbot a higher score as
applicant for a =
position of =E2=80=9Cgeneral-all-round-teacher=E2=80=9D
over Hawking. =
Why not then generate an "astronaut robot" from
http://www.lely.com =
which has a prominent presence in BC, assembled to look
exactly like =
Hawking? Hawkingbot as 5-13 can also milk cows far
better than the real =
Professor Hawking. Lely cow-milking robots are the
leading marketed =
product for that global high tech firm but they do far
more than milk =
cows. They gather and dispense knowledge and in that
sense they practice =
epistemology. Presently there is no high demand for cow

milkers in space =
though a Canadian Moon Colony at the Moon's Mountain of
Eternal Light =
could sustain a troglodyte bovine population. But there
will be a high =
demand for knowledge gathering and dispensing robots in
general when =
Musk et al colonize Moon, Mars and start mining
asteroids in space, all =
of which they will do by the time Canadian babies born
now are young =
adults. This is another reason why Senate and and all
four parties of =
the House of Commons cc'd with this letter should
welcome 5-13 during =
Question Period. How would Canadian civilization itself
be described if =
it were exported to British Columbia and then to a
Canadian Lunar =
Colony? Musk, Branson and other space-farers among the
young billionaire =
leaders of this planet are asking similar questions now.
How shall we =
live in space? A Canadian Catechism generated by
parliamentarians for =
GODBOT can tell the world.

ASK THE EXPERTS!

CHAPTER 1: CANADA'S QUESTION PERIOD

Where wast thou when I laid the foundations of the
Earth? - Job 38:4

It is unfortunate that Prime Minister Chretien and MP
Robinson did not =
carry on with their disagreement about defining the God
of the Canadian =
Constitution during Question Period. But Robot 5-13 can
do this. It can =
educate the world 24/7 without any need for sleep,
feeding or other =
breaks. In doing so, it opens up the way for explaining
to Canadians =
what the entire Constitution of Canada really means.
Let us call this =

opening up of Question Periods our "Patriot Act".
Another wise saying of =
Prime Minister Chretien's was "The Constitution belongs
to the people". =
GODBOT can open up an Internet line to all 35,000,000
present Canadians. =
Aristotle said "If liberty and equality, as is thought
by some, are =
chiefly to be found in democracy, they will be best
attained when all =
persons alike share in the government to the utmost".
It is unfortunate =
that the now-defunct Reform Party did not take on the
responsibility to =
lead the small group involvements at the constituency
level which would =
have been necessary for Aristotelean politics to
succeed. Even Sociology =
100 tells us the organizing and leadership which starts
with a =
constituency of about 100,000 having an MP must descend
to the grass =
roots level. For example "10" could be the unit of
political organizing. =
10 -> 100 -> 1,000 -> 10,000 -> 100,000. "Reform" was
doomed to failure =
even before it elected one of its many MPs. Question
Period would have =
had to reach the grass roots level for it to succeed.
How would the =
three wise men of the west, Socrates, Plato and
Aristotle, use =
=E2=80=9CSocratic Dialogue=E2=80=9D to program GODBOT
compared to the =
three wise men from the east in the Gospel Story? Are
there any =
philosophers with expertise in Socratic methods who can
answer that?

A Cambridge 5-13 robot according to job description
must teach =
epistemology and metaphysics. Epistemology has to do
with knowledge in =
general. Let us then start the 5-13 grammatical program
in C computer =
language grammar with the KNOWLEDGE OF METAPHYSICS.
What could be more =

general than metaphysics which is above, beyond ... on top of the whole =
wide world? Metaphysics has to do with transcendence or ineffability =
Job 38:4 is an example. If those =E2=80=9Cfoundations=E2=80=9D refer to =
a Big Bang-like event, there is no time/place in our terms which =
precedes it. Job 38:4 is ineffable. And now, for the first time in =
history, ineffability has come into the science lab via quantum studies. =
Poetically, in the popular song lyrics of The Carpenters:

I'm on top of the world, looking down on creation;
And the only explanation I can find, is the love that I found, ever =
since You've been around,
Your love's put me on the top of the world.

The books of the Bible are recognized by billions of Jews, Catholics, =
Protestants and Christians who are not Catholics or Protestants as well =
as Muslims and others (even some Buddhists and Hindus) as carrying an =
amazing revelation of metaphysics. This revelation comes in the form of =
grammatical First Person words from God which some Bibles set out in Red =
Letters. Red Letter words have a grammatical form which is in essence, I =
am God and I say _______________. These are put forward in print as the =
direct words of God in contrast with indirect black letter words which =
are commentary on the direct words and deeds of God. Words however do =
not suffice to express how awesome this Biblical claim is and it is an =
awesome claim even to those who reject the validity of the words. The =
claim is this:

* *
* * * * * * * * * * * * * * * * =

```
****************************************************************
******************=
****************************************************************
*****************=
*********************************************
```

God, who is ineffable by definition and transcends all creation =
including the creation of words and the creation of billions of galaxies =
x billions of stars has occasionally spoken directly to people on this =
planet.

```
****************************************************************
******************=
****************************************************************
*****************=
****************************************************************
*****************=
********************************************
```

Metaphysics by bare bones definition does not have to be personal. The =
metaphysical realm does not have to be populated. However the sacred =
tradition of the Hebrew people was that the Almighty is metaphysical but =
could also be physically manifested. He could speak through and even =
become a flesh-and-blood or other physically incarnated manifestation. =
God speaks to Job and his friends through the whirlwind. God speaks to =
Moses "out of the mountain" (Exodus 19:3). In Exodus 20:21 Moses nears =
the "thick darkness" which is "where God was". In Exodus 3:2 the "Angel =
of the Lord" appeared to Moses "in a flame of fire" which is "in the =
midst of the thorn bush". Since we read in Exodus 3:4 that God CALLS to =
Moses out of the midst of the thorn bush, either the Angel of the Lord =
is God the Holy Spirit or a lesser angel and given the grammar it is =
reasonable to understand this as God the Holy Spirit. That is how Moses =
understood his Red Letter, audible-verbal encounters

with God though =
God says in Exodus 33:20 "You cannot see My face". In Exodus 33:9-10 we =
read that "the cloudy pillar descended and stood at the door of the =
tabernacle". God spoke with Moses and "all the people saw the cloudy =
pillar". In the last chapter of Exodus (38) we read that the cloud was =
upon the tabernacle by day and the fire by night were in the sight of =
ALL the House of Israel. When the cloud was taken up the Hebrew nomads =
journeyed on. All means 600,000 according to "Essential Judaism: A =
Complete Guide to Beliefs, Customs, and Rituals" (page 431) by George =
Robinson. The pillar cloud was specifically seen by Aaron, brother of =
Moses and his wife Miriam in Numbers 12:5 where we read that the Lord =
came down in that cloud -that means He was physically manifested to =
human beings through the cloud. Sometimes God is said to be present IN =
these physical objects and sometimes the objects are signs ASSOCIATED =
with His presence. The carnal (flesh and blood) manifestation of God is =
indicated in other passages. Who was the MAN worshipped by Joshua as God =
in Joshua 5:13-15? Who was the MAN who wrestled with Jacob in Genesis =
32:24, who then blessed Jacob and gave him the new name and title of =
Israel whereby he is said to have power with both God and humankind? =
This thread of God being the ineffable God (purely metaphysical or =
purely spiritual) and also manifested as Man is very clear in the Old =
Testament and it is carried forward to New Testament. Experts in =
religion use such passages to find support for New Testament Holy =
Trinity teaching in the Old Testament. Experts in quantum science will =

see the analogy in quantum science where A can be both A and not-A at =
the same time. This is elaborated in the Rock Hunter book, "The Jew Who =
Said He Was God" (TJWSHWG).=20

It is likewise according to the sacred teaching authority of the Hebrew =
people which may be oral or written that God who is spirit was also =
physically manifested in various ways as above. The primary reference =
for teaching and tradition is sacred scripture so these are the three =
inter-related pillars on which Judaism stands: sacred tradition, sacred =
teaching and sacred scripture. But "Judaism has never called for an =
unreasoning faith" we read in the De Sola Poole Traditional Jewish =
Prayer Book and Jews of all denominations could be expected to be very =
receptive to questions and answers through GODBOT. "Judaism is one ... =
denominations are many" (Jewish Almanac, 1980, page 504). On the other =
hand blind dogmatists, bigots and fanatics are anathema to good, honest =
questions. What competent religionist would not welcome questions about =
the Red Letter God of the Bible? How will MPs and Senators relate to =
GODBOT on Parliament Hill during Question Period? It needs repeating =
that GODBOT is programmed with a series of ESPs (Expert System Programs) =
put in place by experts and these are followed by Q-A sets, also =
prepared by experts. The present writing is only a treatise on the =
grammatical framework for GODBOT. Any and all particulars are left to =
experts. GODBOT is the space age electronic blank page on which the =
experts can write their political-religious catechisms (highly =
authoritative works). The present writing does not put

material on those =
pages.

A number of Red Letter question and answer (Q-A) sets are found in the =
Bible. Those who see the Hebrew Bible as sacred scripture will =
understand this well. Abraham questions God about the destruction of =
Sodom and Gomorrhah in Genesis Chapter 18. Joshua asks God if He is for =
the Israelites or their foes (Joshua 5:13). Gideon asks this question =
and others in Judges 6:13. God questions Job and his friends about the =
limitations of their knowledge ... human knowledge. David questions God =
about his battle with the Philistines in I Chronicles Chapter 14; also I =
Samuel 23:2 and 30:8. God answers clearly. TJWSHWG engaged in various =
New Testament Q-A sessions. Reasoning and proof/testing are very much a =
Biblical mainstay and critics who claim the Bible is irrational should =
read more closely. In Red Letters we read "Let us reason together" =
(Isaiah 1:18) and in black letter commentary, "Prove all things" (I =
Thess. 5:21). It is hard to imagine arriving at proof of a case by =
reason in any court, secular or religious without questions and answers. =
What then is the argument against programming GODBOT as a highly =
authoritative teaching machine for many subjects? It cannot be any more =
heretical to install those words in GODBOT than to install them in a =
Xulon You Tube or print publication; or to present them by various high =
technology means in the God Quad at Notre Dame.

ASK THE EXPERTS!

CHAPTER 2: C FOR CANADIAN?

Is it not for you to know judgement? Who hate the good
and love the evil =
.... - Micah 3:2-3

The late Prime Minister Trudeau chose justice and the
"Just Society" as =
his banner. He closes his chapter in "Toward A Just
Society" (1990) with =
a poetic and metaphysical expression. We read that "our
Great Helmsman =
is indeed steering Canada toward peace and
reconciliation - the kind to =
be found in the graveyards of the deep" (page 385).
Perhaps he foresaw =
the imminent and inevitable balkanization of Canada.
Yet every end is a =
new beginning.

Any computing or machine language is a grammar and
prima facie it is as =
value-neutral as a blank piece of paper. It does not
advocate any =
ideology, religion, doctrine or belief system. That is
the =
responsibility of experts in the related fields. An AI
like 5-13 has a =
tabula rasa machine "brain" upon which anything can be
written. That =
should appeal to Parliamentarians who champion equality
rights in =
Charter section 15. S.15 does not however deny anyone
the opportunity to =
prove ideological superiority. S.15 is like the
starting gate in a horse =
race. It gives all an equal chance in the race but not
an equal chance =
to win.

To program robot 5-13 with Red Letter monologue-
lectures from Genesis to =
Revelation is easy. In fact all of C programming and
other computer =
programming is easy. High technology people seem to
work hard at keeping =
this knowledge from the public. The present GODBOT
treatise makes the =
point that educational robotics will soon put an end to

exploitation of =
the uneducated as we see in popularized computing. But the general plan =
is also found in various Yahoo lists as in the cc field of this "Love =
Letter to Parliament": example, C-and-SEE. Computer languages are =
complex but easy just as a chess C program is complex and easy (easily =
applied). With a sufficiently powerful computer brain, 5-13 will not =
lose a chess game to anyone. With ease it defeats all adversaries. With =
the correct C program, written by experts it can answer questions about =
Red Letter metaphysics better than any single human expert when it is =
programmed by many experts and by the best of those experts ... the best =
of the best. As Hawking's robotic twin it will teach math-physics better =
than Hawking. Why then would sensible and thrifty students not enroll in =
a 5-13 class at minimal cost rather than an expensive Hawking class?

Consider C as a grammar which can be used (responded to as if =
understood) by the machine. The units of this grammar are called =
functions by Prata in his 2002 text, C Primer Plus. On page 301 he says =
"C's design philosophy is to use functions as building blocks" and "A =
function is a self-contained unit of program code designed to accomplish =
a particular task". In other words, C grammar is a language of the =
machine which tells the machine what to do. Pertainiing to the present =
task of 5-13, Prata writes "For example, printf() causes data to be =
printed on your screen". The particular characters required to use =
printf() can be asked of any C expert or located in a text like Prata's. =
A print statement in C can be used to encapsulate any

monologue/lecture. =
Off-the-shelf software can be installed to have 5-13
turn the print into =
oral expression as Hawking's voice synthesizer does.=20

The standard educational procedure entails a
monologue/lecture followed =
by Q-A sessions with students. Law makers proceed the
same way with =
legislation, executive decisions and other matters of
importance to =
public administration followed by Question Period.
After printf() delivers the lecture, another function
can be used so =
that 5-13 does the opposite. Instead of an output of
words (more =
broadly, characters) it inputs the audience or student
questions. The =
functions necessary for this are found in Prata's
Chapter 4 titled =
"Character Strings and Formatted Input/Output" as well
as other =
chapters. C's grammatical functions can instruct 5-13
to read print as =
well as type print. Student questions can be presented
through =
off-the-shelf software which turns oral questioning
into print. After =
that, functions like getchar() will input
characters/words of student =
questions to 5-13 so that it can respond with answers.

Programmers will carry on with the "design philosophy"
(to use Prata's =
expression) for 5-13 as an epistemological machine
which is amenable to =
all questions and answers of interest to
parliamentarians in Canada and =
beyond.

ASK THE EXPERTS!

CHAPTER 3: A CANADIAN RENAISSANCE

Art thou (Nicodemus) a master of Israel and knowest not
these things? - =
John 3:10

In the passage above, TJWSHWG is speaking to a Jewish Pharisee leader =
who recognizes Jesus as a "rabbi", a "a teacher come from God" because =
of the miracles (John 3:2) but Nicodemus had yet to recognize the =
miracle of renaissance which is rebirth. A Canadian Renaissance, defined =
as a rebirth of civilization is imminent. When we consider how Canadians =
might live on the Moon over the next few decades we will inevitably =
reconsider how they live here.

The first Red Letter words of the Bible are "Let there be light". These =
four words may be accompanied in a C program with corresponding black =
letter commentary. After that lecture, there will be student questions. =
It is the human experts who will initially answer those questions. Their =
answers are then programmed into 5-13 by C programmers who may use C "if =
statements". In Prata (page 221) we read, "The if statement is called a =
branching statement or selection statement because it provides a =
junction where the program has to select which of two paths to =
follow".The general form given is

if (expression)
        statement=20

If students ask a certain question pertaining to the fiat lux lecture =
such as "What is light?" then 5-13 will respond ___________ where the =
blank is filled in by human experts. Experienced college lecturers will =
say that after giving a course so many times, they are rarely surprised =
by a new student question. "What is light?" and similar questions will =
be grouped and any variation in that group will evoke

the same answer =
from GODBOT. Questions of this nature will lead to answers about literal =
and metaphorical uses of the word light. Literal questions may even deal =
with the physics of light. Why does e =3D mc2 and not mc3? Where is =
there a nuclear reactor anywhere on this planet with data to answer the =
question? If they are not forthcoming with the information, why is that?

The programming technology for Q-A sessions is the same as that used by =
Google and other search engines. The words/characters we insert into the =
search engine are essentially questions. Two words: "question" and =
"period", give similar results or answers to the question "What is =
Question Period?" But the important difference for educational purposes =
has to do with "human equivalency". Since 5-13 (aka GODBOT or =
Hawkingbot) as a Hawking-lookalike is performing like the real Hawking =
lecturer, it will be accepted by students whereas non-humanoid teaching =
machines are not accepted. Moreover, thousands of subjects can be taught =
this way and at very low cost. (Read again the trillion dollar student =
debt above - and that is US only). The initial cost of C programming is =
mostly related to grouping the questions after each lecture and linking =
them by if-then code as above to the best answers. Given the success of =
pro bono public education through wiki and related projects, one would =
expect many volunteer experts to come forward and provide this =
assistance. Thousands of sets of course materials gathered from hundreds =
of universities by MIT since 2001 in a project called OCW (Open =
Courseware) have no value unless they are taught. They

can be taught by =
5-13.

The metaphysics lesson on light becomes an educational
enlightenment in =
the broadest sense. The Cambridge job description
requires teaching of =
epistemology as well as metaphysics. Since 5-13 can
teach knowledge in =
thousands of subjects, it meets that requirement. It is
a =
metaphysics-epistemology-teaching robot, a God Tube
robot and it sets a =
"new direction in (artificial) mind" which is also part
of the Cambridge =
job description. If Cambridge does not want to hire
Hawkingbot, perhaps =
Oxford does. The English who led the Industrial
Revolution must be =
tempted to lead the Robot Revolution.

ASK THE EXPERTS!

CHAPTER 4: RED LETTER CANADIAN PRINCIPLES

Come now, and let us reason together ... though your
sins be as scarlet, =
they shall be as white as snow - Isaiah 1:18
=20

The three pillars of Israelite faith are presented in
Chapter 1. Before =
the Israelites were given the sacred teaching authority
of the Decalogue =
or Ten Commandments they lived under Egyptian dominion
without this =
revelation. During those centuries, the population
expanded from the =
extended family of Jacob (Israel) to 600,000 migrating
people at Mount =
Sinai. Sacred teaching was associated with supporting
sacred traditions =
(customs, rituals, rites etc) and sacred writings ...
the Bible. =
Robinson says "The Bible is a book with many names, as
befits a work =
that is protean in form and cosmic in scope" (page 257).

He refers to it =
as the "Hebrew Bible" listing its 39 booklets from
Genesis to II =
Chronicles on pages 258-259. Robinson does not
recognize the New =
Testament booklets like the book titled "Hebrews". One
might ask his =
religious authorities to reason out what is
objectionable about Hebrews? =
Why does it not describe the perfect Hebrew sacrifice
... the perfect =
and unforgettable offering?

Sacred writings/teachings are passed on over hundreds
and thousands of =
years and they constitute sacred tradition of
themselves along with =
associated acts. They may be passed on ritualistically
and with ceremony =
as part of other sacred traditions. The Decalogue is
supported by all =
three sacred pillars. Israelite teaching authorities
must therefore be =
very upset by any diminution, alteration or desecration
of the Ten =
Commandments. Parliament serves a Constitution which is
"founded upon =
principles" as we read in the Canadian Charter of
Rights and Freedoms. =
The Ten Commandments pertain to TEN important
principles. Each is =
distinct and very clearly and easily differentiated
from any other. They =
cannot be fused together or conflated, nor can any one
be artificially =
split up or dissembled. They can of course be
summarized as the general =
title (Decalogue or Ten Commandments) is a
summarization.

Given that the courts of Canada have defined the
"supremacy of God =
clause" in our Constitution as Canadian highest
principles, the TEN =
PRINCIPLES of the Ten Commandments must be of great
interest to =
law-makers. They must also ask what the so-called

"Traditional =
Catechetical Formula" for the Decalogue does to its
meaning. Refer to =
paragraphs 2051-2052 of Catechism of the Catholic
Church, Pope John Paul =
II (Karl Josef Wojtyla) edition. The First Commandment
of the =
traditional (and sacred) Israelite phrasing is fused
with the second, =
rendering them one command. This fusion/conflation
creates confusion. =
The God of the Hebrews is not an author of confusion (a
question per se =
is not a confusion). The sacred Israelite First
Commandment is analogous =
to an "Order in the Court" proclamation. But this
Commandment does =
infinitely more. It commands and demands that the
metaphysical realm be =
recognized as more than a universal or mother nature
machine. The =
universe has a PERSONAL CREATOR. Canadians of course
are free by law to =
disagree with that. The Second Command or Principle is
that "You shall =
have no other gods before me". It is clearly not the
same as the First. =
With equal confusion, the Traditional Catechetical
Formula takes the =
Tenth Commandment "Thou shalt not covet _______" and
turns it into two =
separate commands by giving two examples of
covetousness. That becomes =
extremely questionable also by elementary logic. If two
examples create =
two Commandments, why are there not 200 or 2,000
Commandments? Of course =
the Bible carries many orders and directives from God.
But there are =
only TEN primary Commandments which can be SUMMARIZED
(not conflated or =
dissembled) in the Summary of the Law. The Baptist
"Traditional =
Catechetical Formula" is also available online and it
too rephrases the =
Decalogue in ways which detract from its clear and
distinct ten =

principles.

What do Ten Principles have to do with Question Period? EVERYTHING. =
"Canada is founded upon principles that recognize the supremacy of God". =
Perhaps that is the deeper cause of Nielsen's polemical book: He writes =
as if he was denied the right or power or opportunity to ask good, =
honest questions about those fundamental principles of Canadian =
civilization ... the principles that Canadians would want to export to =
secessionist BC and from there to the Moon as BC First Nations prepare =
to uncouple BC from Canada. As parliamentarians write the new Catechism =
of Canada for those "highest principles" in a model civilization located =
in BC what will it be like? How will it read? This is a huge =
responsibility for parliamentary experts. Since any political-religious =
catechism presents itself as HIGHLY authoritative, the entire =
presentation becomes suspect when a major untruth is discovered.=20

Robson refers to "The Almighty" repeatedly in his book and recognizes =
the many names for The Almighty. The word Almighty means all-powerful. =
An all-powerful Deity by definition has all power over knowledge and =
ignorance; all power over perfection and imperfection; all power over =
good and evil. Traditions, even sacred traditions, do indeed change. The =
"Golden Calf Rebellion" was crushed by the Israelite authorities who =
were led by Moses with support of his Levite clan. They slaughtered =
thousands of fellow Israelites for violating the Second Commandment. It =
is difficult to imagine modern Israel doing this when Prime Minister =

Golda Meier once lamented the problem of national cohesiveness in a =
nation with one third Atheist believers. Atheism rejects the First =
Commandment. Moses would not have spared the life of anyone calling him =
or God a liar as Atheistic Jews do. Perhaps by recognizing the change in =
sacred traditions over the centuries we can explain Roman Catholicism's =
catechetical deviation from the sacred tradition of the Israelite =
teaching authority. In what century was this new Decalogue "formula" =
invented? What other questionable statements, questionable formulas and =
untruths might one find in Catholic Catechism or the Protestant =
Catechisms? When did Israelite civiilzation recognize Atheism as a valid =
Israelite belief system? When did it start to deny the teachings of =
TJWSHWG as the Israelite way forward when the New Testament Bible refers =
repeatedly to followers of TJWSHWG as Israelites/Judahites and Jews and =
only three times as "Christians"?

So many questions arise when good, honest, principled people discuss =
principles. Fortunately there are experts to answer which rules out =
bigots (the dead who bury the dead) and blind dogmatists (the blind who =
lead the blind). Experts in the principles of God are not prejudiced =
people who pre-judge the statements of others and call them heretical =
without justification. The Question Period of Parliament according to =
GODBOT's catechetical formula becomes a political-religious activity. =
How could it be otherwise? Highest principles are highest principles no =
matter who puts them forward and no matter what their vocation.

ASK THE EXPERTS!

CHAPTER 5: PEACE, ORDER AND GOOD CANADIAN GOVERNMENT

Be still and know that I am God - Psalms 46:10

The Red Letter expression above sounds like a Hindu or Zen Buddhist =
mantra (which instructs the stilling of the mind). The monotheistic =
teachings of the patriarchs in Babylon preceded Hinduism and Buddhism as =
well as the religions of Ancient China. Absolute knowledge came to =
Elijah, not in the great wind or the rocks or earthquake or fire but in =
"a still, small voice" (I Kings 19:12) and that still, small voice of =
God posed a question to Elijah, "What are you doing here?" The great =
swelling words and words as shallow as sounding brass (Biblical =
expressions) which emanate from political-religious frauds do not answer =
that simple and sound question from God. What are parliamentarians doing =
here? What are millions of popes, priests and preachers doing here? What =
are typical Canadians doing here and can we do better by designing a =
CANOPOLIS well?

The phrase "peace, order and good government" can be accessed by www =
search and is often used in parliamentary systems. Who are the experts =
in spelling out the meaning of "good" as a comprehensive way of life ... =
a civilization, for this planet and beyond? Though an Almighty God by =
definition (and by reality to believers) has full power over all good =
and evil, the Bible is clear and consistent in Red Letter directives and =
black letter commentary that man is to choose good. Red Letters state =

clearly in Amos 5:15 "Hate the evil, and love the
good_____". Red =
Letters ask Solomon to make a request. In I Kings 3:5,
Solomon asks "to =
discern between good and bad" and his wish is granted.
Popular knowledge =
is "the wisdom of Solomon". But Biblical passages
subordinate wisdom to =
"love the good" and for believers that must lead to God
as the creator =
of all that is good. We read that the wisdom of man is
foolishness to =
God. Solomon also did not ask for righteousness as we
read that there is =
none righteous, no not one. What then do we say of
those who claim to be =
holy or pious in their righteousness? Hollywood has no
difficulty =
finding actors to play the roles of religionists who
make such claims =
for themselves. Solomon's request sounds as simple as a
child's =
Christmas wish. But it was honest and sound and it was
granted. That was =
the wisdom of Solomon and one might argue that it was
even on a higher =
level than what we usually call wisdom since good-bad
originates =
metaphysically. There is no physical formula for good-
bad.

If we ask the religion masters, why not start with
those who are experts =
in the Hebrew Bible which presents the idealization of
civilization =
beginning with Eden and continuing through the
centuries with the =
struggles of the Israelites toward establishing their
idealized "Kingdom =
of God" on this planet? T.J. Wray writes in her text,
"What The Bible =
Really Tells Us" (WTBRTU) that Heaven should be
differentiated from =
Kingdom of Heaven or Kingdom of God. She calls the
Christian Bible which =
she uses a "Hebrew Bible" which is generically correct.
All Christian =

Bibles are Hebrew Bibles. The New Testament carries forward Old =
Testament teachings. It does not revoke them. We read on page 108 that =
Heaven "should not be confused with what Jesus calls the Kingdom of God, =
sometimes rendered the Kingdom of Heaven in the Gospel of Matthew, which =
refers to an earthly reality". A most important 'rendering' is in The =
Lord's Prayer (the only formal prayer given by TJWSHWG). Since billions =
of Christians have prayed in The Lord's Prayer for the establishing of a =
materially observable civilization of God on this planet, should =
Parliament not be bringing the experts of Christian religion into =
Parliament for Question Period and the programming of GODBOT? Do they =
know how to articulate "good" as in "good, better and best"? Perhaps =
Professor Wray (Salve Regina University) can tell us in her next text =
What The Bible Really Tells Us About The Hebrew Ideal Civilization.

Why not ask the Jews in Canada's multicultural mosaic to write such a =
script since most of the Old Testament is about the ongoing Red Letter =
communications between the Almighty and His Chosen People toward the =
objective of establishing a priestly nation of priestly people, living =
IHS (In His Service) 24/7? A complication of this matter is presented by =
Asimov in his book titled "Asimov's Guide To The Bible: The Old =
Testament". He says that "The united kingdom over which David thus came =
to rule in 1006 BC is called Israel in the Bible, but the kingdom was =
never really single. The two halves of the nation were never truly =
amalgamated" (page 301). The kingdom called Judah and that called Israel =

each had its own king line. They were usually in conflict and sometimes =
at war with one another. Judah was populated by descendants of the sons =
of Jacob: Judah and Benjamin. Israel was populated by descendants of =
Gad, Dan, Zebullon, Joseph and the other sons of Jacob. Levites, as the =
priestly clan could live in either kingdom. This sacred tradition of the =
Israelites continues today in Christendom since the priesthood of the =
same Christian denomination may be located in two countries engaged in =
bitter warfare. Asimov writes on page 95 that "While members of all =
twelve tribes are Israelites, it is the members of the tribe of Judah =
only that are, strictly speaking, Judeans or Jews". In this context the =
point made by some Bible scholars that the word "Jew" was a later =
introduction to the Bible, replacing Judean or Judahite is irrelevant. =
In the New Testament, a list can be made of all references to Jew and =
Israelite to show that the two words are used interchangeably. St. Paul, =
aka Saul, correctly refers to himself as "the Jew of Tarsus" and also as =
an Israelite of the tribe of Benjamin.

A man's reach must exceed his grasp, or what's a heaven for said the =
poet Blake. In Red Letters we read in Acts 7:49 that Heaven is God's =
throne and earth is His footstool. "What house will you build me?" asks =
the Lord. And though we also read in the Red Letters of Isaiah 55:8-9 =
that "My ways are higher than your ways and My thoughts are higher than =
your thoughts", the question is not merely rhetorical. In Exodus 31:2 =
God tells Moses He has "called by name Bezaleel" (Tribe of Judah) and =
given Bezaleel knowledge in all workmanship as the

chief builder in the =
Israelite Kingdom of God. Despite His higher ways, God interacts with =
humankind in this world. That is what the Bible is about. As Asimov =
writes, "The most influential, the most published, the most widely read =
book in the history of the world is the Bible" (page 9).=20

Ottawa's Parliament, therefore, as the multicultural "Parliament of =
Nations" has already invited all religions or belief systems from A-Z, =
Atheist to Zoroastrian, to articulate the ideals of their civilization. =
Why not spell it out for export to Moon, Mars and beyond?=20

Parliament may want to start by spelling out what Canadian civilization =
is like for export from Ottawa to Indian land in British Columbia. As =
"Gold War: The Lost Gold Mines Of Canada's Indians" by Rock Hunter =
reminds us, BC may be unique in the Western Hemisphere. There never was =
a European colonial claim over BC and there never was an "Indian War" =
whereby the winners might claim ownership of land, paid for in blood. =
The only colonial claim came from Ottawa and it has no foundation in =
international justice. First Nations of BC can walk into the UN General =
Assembly any day and take a seat. Also they can make their claim that =
Ottawa has engaged in ongoing genocide against First Nations people =
across Canada, proven by extrapolation from the Frank Paul case and =
Gosselin case (Supreme Court of Canada, 2001). Succintly, one must ask =
what would have happened if Paul rather than Gosselin had appeared =
before SCC. Would Judge McLaughlin et al have said to him as they did to =

Gosselin that Canada has no duty to protect the lives
of citizens when =
they are endangered by homelessness ... and also (as
they did) that it =
costs too much for such justice to prevail? Would they
have said it is =
"justice" to keep putting a series of First Nation
Frank Pauls into =
cold, wet streets by police action which caused Frank
to die of =
exposure? If so, that demographic differential would
cause the death =
and destruction of more First Nation people than
average and such a =
differential/discriminatory administration would be
genocidal. Yet the =
McLaughlin SCC declared this to be justice. The
Criminal Code of Canada =
pertaining to genocide can be read online. By bizarre
and false =
"reasoning" McLaughlin and her majority of 5 (v the
minority of 4) =
asserted in effect that justice in Canada would not
come from her court =
unless it was cheap. She said that it would cost too
much to provide the =
essentials for life to the mentally ill and the native
people who, in =
combination are the majority of the homeless in Canada.
Yet a generation =
before her, homelessness was almost unknown in this
country and much =
more expensive institutions housed and fed the mentally
ill. Thus =
McLaughlin effectively (though probably unknowingly)
made a pompous =
declaration in defense of what Hitler called "useless
eaters" policy. In =
this case the useless eaters subjected to Canadian
genocide rather than =
the Hitlerian variety are those with clearly defined
demographics: poor =
and native.=20

The ideal of Canadian civilization is not genocidal and
one must wonder, =
parenthetically if recall of judges like SCC judges

would solve the =
problem? How will that model, exported from Ottawa to BC, deal with =
homeless First Nations people? Will they be subjected to ongoing =
homelessness-related killing conditions in the present differential way? =
What would that civilization be like, exported to Indian land in BC and =
thence off-planet? What would a model of Jewish civilization by =
comparison be like? American civilization? Chinese civilization? China =
Towns are well liked across Canada. What would a China City (of perhaps =
100,000) be like? Here in BC we can let 1,000 flowers of =
multicullturalism bloom, paid for in gold as BC becomes the new South =
Africa of precious metal mining. Refer to "Gold War". Canadian =
civilization is not only good but the best of the best because =
________________. Spell this out for BC, feature by feature. If it is the =
best of the best, we British Columbians can export it off-planet.

ASK THE EXPERTS!

CHAPTER 6: GOOD, BETTER AND BEST IN CANADA

Hate the evil and love the good - Amos 5:15

BC wants to export the best of the best off-planet. Earth would probably =
import precious metals from off-planet British Columbian colonies since =
D.K. Yeomans tells us in his book, "Near-Earth Objects" (2013) that a =
one km wide rocky asteroid contains TRILLIONS of dollars in precious =
metals. "Irons" or metallic asteroids contain more. There are tens of =
thousands of trillion dollar asteroids in surface and near surface =

deposits of Moon and Mars where the organic regolith (overburden) to =
block access does not exist. Imagine how much mineral wealth would be =
discovered if BC, twice the area of Japan and over 90% mountainous, were =
devoid of organic overburden. On Mars the extreme winds blow gold, =
silver and platinum placer deposits into crater and canyon traps even =
though the atmosphere is very thin. Also they lay bare the bedrock as =
they move on to other locations. Though the atmosphere is very thin and =
weak, it still yields enormous formations of sand dunes and dust dunes. =
Both are easily located and surface placer deposits of gold, silver and =
platinums abound. On Moon, the loose sediments of the surface are very =
shallow, enabling easy geophysical penetration and mapping. Why mine the =
asteroids which are loose, astrogeological sedimentary floats in space =
when the asteroids are found on Moon and Mars in abundance and can be =
mined by mining colonies of former Earthlings? Media should ask Senator =
Neufeld (former mining minister in BC) about Canadian Moon and Mars =
mining. Ask a good, honest question of a Canadian in Parliament and =
________________?

Canada does not own the land or mineral deposits or any other natural =
resource of BC. Ask Senator Sibbeston this good, honest question. But it =
can claim jurisdiction over present off-reservation personnel. When =
those personnel are living on reservations and the social order is =
reversed in that sense, applications may be made to a First Nation Space =
City. Who are the "best of the best" to use a Donald Trump slogan? All =
of the cultures of multiculturalism are not equal any

more than all =
religions are equal. Some are quite banal. Some are
"terrorist" in =
nature. Some are evil, plain and simple, although we
tend to call these =
social-political-religious evils "cults" rather than
cultures. The =
Procult Institute of Vancouver was formed by close
advisors to former BC =
Premier Vanderzalm to advance the cults of Canada with
its flagship tome =
titled "Stop Apologizing" (1991) by J Cyllorn. MPs in
Ottawa at the =
time took umbrage at Cyllorn's magnum opus. Robert Lee
published in the =
Vancouver Sun that "a number of MPs wanted J Cyllorn
prosecuted for =
hate-mongering" and that Cyllorn was "(Premier) Bill
Vander Zalms's =
one-time numerologist". This ceased when they realized
that Madame =
Cyllorn still read the tea leaf futures of Premier
"Bill V", projecting =
numbers onto them in a bizarre practice of superstition
which once =
earned him the headline story of the Vancouver Sun
daily newspaper.

Protestants may enter the BC competition of cultures
but Protestantism =
is merely a branch from Catholicism. Judaic
Christianity on the other =
hand preceded both so they are branches from the "True
Vine" of the Lion =
of Judah. The Modern King James Version Of The Holy
Bible by Jay P. =
Green, Sr. goes further with its wording when it says,
"Behold, days are =
coming says the Lord, and I will make an end on the
house of Israel, and =
on the house of Judah a new covenant shall be" (Hebrews,
8:8). This =
wording may be seen by some as a questionable
restatement but TJWSHWG is =
most certainly described as from the Judahite lineage
and the final Red =
Letter words of the Bible are "I am the root and the

offspring of David, =
the bright and morning star". King David was of course
a Judahite. Thus =
we see an elaboration on the original C program fiat
lux lesson. Where =
does light (as in star light?) differ from literal
light? Is it only =
metaphor when Revelation refers to an angel standing in
the light of the =
Sun?

What is the greatest heartfelt desire of humankind? It
people are given =
just one wish, what will it be? Whether it is called
Heaven, Kingdom of =
Heaven or Paradise, surely to live in a state which
expresses goodness =
to the greatest degree, protected forever from harm
would sum that up. =
That perfection would apply within each person and it
would apply to the =
surroundings. Can the Pax Canadiana provide the
protection? Prudential =
funded the Westlake Hills, California development in
the 1970s and used =
the slogan "Paradise at a Price" for advertising. It is
not merely =
utopian hot air. Every developer will claim to be
"doing the best I can" =
whether the project is to to expand an existing
settlement or build one =
totally anew. The word "good"is central or foundational.
Take it feature =
by feature: ________________ is a good feature because
____________________. =
We pursue that which is good within ourselves and in
our surroundings. =
That formula is simple and true.

TJWSHWG said "Seek ye first the Kingdom of Heaven".
With what =
consequence? "All these things will be added to you".
The experts of all =
religions teach and preach how to live. How would they
reply to the =
questioning of a Question Period about the model
civilization for one =

and all, 24/7, on and off planet? The Future Canada for babies born now =
will include off-planet habitation as an option. Therefore it is far =
from vain imagining to ask what it might be like in a BC Future city =
designed now. We ask the experts in hundreds of fields. Each of us is =
like the blind men feeling different parts of the elephant and wondering =
what it is. By pooling notes, the identity can be made. A civilization =
is not the project of one person. The simple formula becomes complex but =
still easily understood when experts are required to communicate in =
standard everyday English (SEE). SEE in hundreds or thousands of =
specializations becomes a C program. The task of MPs and Senators is to =
make sure the experts translate their technical terminology into SEE.

ASK THE EXPERTS!

CHAPTER 7: THE TRADITIONAL CANADIAN CATECHETICAL FORMULA

Call to me, and I will answer thee, and show thee great and mighty =
things which, which thou knowest not - Jeremiah 33:3

If the God of the Canadian Constitution (Supremacy of God Clause) is the =
one true God, why would the above not apply to those who seek His =
directives toward a better future for citizens of the space age which =
has just begun? In the case of this country though we must recognize =
that we are re-defining Canadianism as soon as we start to colonize =
off-planet ... or even think about it. That is how BC will be especially =
but enigmatically helpful. To explain better consider a colony of, let =
us say 100,000 Canadians on Moon or Mars. They will be

or become =
self-sufficient by necessity. By generally accepted space law, no nation =
can claim sovereignty off-planet. But privacy rights prevent intrusions =
to the colonial living space. The inhabitants are self-sufficient, =
autonomous Moonlings or Martians. Nothing mandates that they identify =
themselves as Canadians or serve Canada beyond any commercial debts but =
their Canadian origin will identify them factually as Neo-Canadians. For =
Ottawa to recognize that BC has never lawfully been part of Canada =
allows Canadians a chance to redefine themselves before exporting this =
model of civilization at its best into space.

The Old Testament is largely a dialogue with commentary between the =
Almighty God and His Chosen People. What is its objective? The objective =
is to re-establish an idealized state of existence for humankind on this =
planet. The dialogue starts with Eden and that ideal state. It is lost =
when Adam and Eve yield to the temptation to know evil as well as good =
which otherwise was their life 24/7. Genesis takes us through the trials =
of the patriarchs after that up to Jacob/Israel. Then we have book after =
book of the struggles of the Israelites with the task of re-establishing =
an idealized state, a way of life for thousands or millions of people, =
not Adam and Eve alone. The narrow definition of Zionism is the =
establishing of Israelite civilization around Mt Zion in Jerusalem but =
the broad definition is the establishing of an idealized civilization =
for all who want it. The Tribe/Nation of Judah became the world's =
largest adoption agency.=20

Any person of sound mind will seek an idealized way of life, a way of =
life which is good, better and best. Epstein wrote in the scholarly =
journal "Judaism" circa 1980 that Judaism, contrary to popular belief is =
a proselytizing religion. He summarizes ten major historical waves of =
proselytizing. Christianity itself is the result of teaching and =
preaching Judaism by TJWSHWG who said not one jot or tittle of the =
Hebrew law was changed by Him.When both the spirit of the law and the =
application of the law are balanced out, this becomes possible. For =
example a letter of the law prohibition against eating shellfish is =
sound when the properties of these creatures are not well known and some =
are poisonous. The spirit of the law has to do with good health and =
other principles. Health knowledge changes the application of the law =
but the law itself does not change. The traditional principles for =
civilization dating back thousands of years applies today and that =
Israelite way of life exists today for all who want it.

Who then are the neo-Israelites? Is the Golden Calf Cult is now accepted =
without censure in modern day Israel? Modern Israel is a nation which =
does not even know the language spoken by the original Israelite (Jacob) =
and his sons in Egypt. They also did not have the Ten Commandments until =
they left Egypt. How then can Israelite civilization be established, =
based on tradition? That can only happen if the PRINCIPLES are adhered =
to (like those of the Decalogue) while the PRACTICES are adapted to time =
and place. Otherwise, do young Canadians today repudiate the Bible and =
God's Law when they venture into mining colonies on the

Moon later in =
this century? What is their description of even one
neo-Israelite =
civilization for BC and export when there could be many?

GOODNESS is a principle. It was chosen by Solomon when
he was told to =
make a choice by God. It is a repeated again and again
in Red Letter and =
black letter writings of the Bible. That summarizing
principle applies =
to all of the particular practices of civilization. We
respect our =
religious ancestors from the ancient world but they
lived under =
primitive conditions with limited knowledge. Primitives
world-wide =
understood blood sacrifice as an offering which they
imagined would =
please those in the hereafter. Just as the Sabbath was
made for man, not =
man for the Sabbath, blood sacrifices were made for man
and not =
vice-versa. In Red Letters we read "Though ye offer me
burnt offerings =
and your meat offerings, I will not accept them" (Amos
5:22). Psalm 40, =
verse 6 tells us "Sacrifice and offering thou didst not
desire". =
Likewise God asks in Psalm 50:13, "Will I eat the
flesh of bulls, or =
drink the blood of goats?" The theme is 100% consistent
that the way of =
life demanded by the Almighty is that which is IHS (In
His Service).

ASK THE EXPERTS!

CHAPTER 8: NOW IS THE TIME, CANADA

Behold, I have put my words in your mouth - Jeremiah
1:9

"Now is the time for all good men to come to the aid of
the Party". That =
used to be the first exercise of multi-digit typing

students just as =
"Hello world!" is the first C programming exercise at
BCIT. What if =
there are no good men to come to the aid of the "Party
of God" and =
program GODBOT? What if there are no good, honest
people to give good, =
honest answers to good, honest questions? What if
Catholic and =
Protestantism catechisms are disingenuous and all these
so-called =
experts who write them can do when asked about a
Christian civilization =
here for export off-planet is evade the questions and
issues? In the =
words of Canadian balladeer Leonard Cohen (CD-The
Future):

Everybody knows the dice were loaded,
Everybody knows the game was rigged,
Everybody knows the good guys lost.
Everybody knows.

We cannot have peace, order and good government unless
there are those =
in leadership positions (parliamentary and religious
institutions) who =
want to end the bad features of civilization in and
around us advance =
the good features. Again, that sounds childlike yet it
was the request =
of King Solomon. There is child-like simplicity in such
a statement but =
the testing of it goes wanting. Are the lyrics of "The
Future" telling =
us something about human nature which political slogans
avoid and =
religion experts flee from? In CCC or Catechism of the
Catholic Church =
(p 801) the reader is told to "test all things" citing
I Thess. 5:12 =
which is similarly stated as "prove all things" in the
KJV Bible =
(hereafter "p" refers to paragraph rather than
page).Upon questioning =
almost all people will say "I am doing my best" when
asked about work =

performance or role in life like parental role. The
GODBOT test is to =
start anew. That is not utopian where utopian connotes
unrealistic or =
pie in the sky. Wilderness preceded all cities today
and the space age =
preparations of this new generation force the planning
of such =
cities/civilizations. A city on the Moon or Mars does
not "just happen". =
Therein we have a proper test for the political-
religious catechism =
experts who claim to be doing their best today for the
current ongoing =
civilization. Will they come forward from Ottawa to
plan a "CANOPOLIS" =
in BC and compete against other models of civilization?
If they flee =
from this p 801 test, they are no experts in the
catechism of a way of =
life. CCC gives an excellent rule for all such experts
regardless of =
their background, politics or religion. If the words of
the experts =
truly come from God, will they say He has put His words
in their mouths? =
Former BC Premier WAC Bennett liked to say, "I am
plugged in to God".

At the time of this writing, billionaire and
presidential candidate =
Donald =E2=80=9Cbest of the best=E2=80=9D Trump is
planning a new office =
tower for Vancouver. If he were to build it as first
structure of a BC =
CANOPOLIS and a replica of Building 7 from the 9/11
horror, that would =
provide an amazing test and a tribute to American
culture, exported to =
Canada, Building 7 according to the official report
tumbled into its own =
basement at almost free-fall speed. Over 90% of it was
pulverized so the =
mass of twisted steel did not occur as expected. The
word =
=E2=80=9Cmiraculous=E2=80=9D is not too strong. This
was reportedly =

caused by =E2=80=9Cmiracle oil=E2=80=9D (jet fuel) spilled onto one =
corner near the top. Trump Tower could have a Building 7 surrogate =
tested before the heavy (red iron) structure is filled in with offices. =
If it can be razed this way, the demolition industry is greatly =
advanced. When it comes time to raze the Trump Tower perhaps a century =
from now, all that has to be done is to pour some miracle oil on it. =
What a cost saving!=20

The UN is a debating club for criminals and despots of the world. The =
ICC might as well be dubbed the International Court of Criminals. UN =
does not even represent the people of its 200 or so nation members and =
ignores THOUSANDS of potential nation members like First Nations across =
Canada, Basques, Kurds, Welsh, Scots and many others. After they are =
liberated from Ottawa's colonialist resource theft, BC First Nations may =
invite any of these foreign nations to provide cultural expression on =
long term leases as Hong Kong once had. BC Indians are mindful of the =
painful history in which their nationhood was only mockingly given =
credence by Ottawa.=20

ASK THE EXPERTS!

CHAPTER 9: QUESTIONS ABOUT THE CANADIAN GOLD WAR

Thy silver and thy gold is mine - I Kings 20:3

Gold War by Rock Hunter was given the ISBN 978-0-9937593-1-4 by the =
Library of Parliament system. It was then published by Xulon Press.

Gold War tells the story of how Frank Paul, a homeless Micmac Indian, =
was killed in Vancouver by what was in effect an extra-judicial =
execution. He was taken from a confining and yet warm and =
health-sustainiing jail cell by VPD and placed in his "home" in an alley =
where (like others before and since) he died of exposure and =
homelessness-related adversity. This fatal result was predictable on a =
probability basis and it is predictable every day in Canada when people =
are forced into conditions of indoor and outdoor homelessness. You might =
call it a Russian-roulette form of Canadian "justice". If Frank had come =
before the McLaughlin Supreme Court in 2001 instead of Louise Gosselin =
one would expect the same result unless the justice system were to =
practice a very strange form of affirmative action. The result would be =
a macabre measure to establish extra-judicial capital punishment ratios =
related to race and gender and ethnicity. Should the judicial system be =
allowed to kill a French Canadian woman (Gosselin) with the same =
alacrity as killing an Indian Canadian man (Paul)?

Demographic parameters are entangled in the thousands of cases of =
homelessness whereby health damaging and life destroying conditions are =
actively forced or passively allowed. Both active and passive factors =
are under the control of governing administrations. Does it exonerate =
these authorities if the demographics are disentangled? The McLaughlin =
et al opinion of 2001 would not deem it unlawful or unjust for a Louise =
Gosselin to be placed in health and life destroying conditions so why =
would it not declare the Frank Paul death to be lawful

and just? If one =
demographic in particular is disentangled (First Nation)
is that no =
longer a clear matter of genocide? The conscience of
Constable Instant =
says otherwise.

Note that there is a SYSTEM of that which is bad/evil
which is being =
decried. Does the political-judicial system of Canada
serves good or =
bad? What does it make of Solomon's choice? Otherwise
______________ is a =
good feature because ___________________. Individuals
like a tearful =
Constable Instant of VPD are not blamed for the death
of Frank Paul. =
They are only following orders in the genocide of the
Indian people and =
poor people of Canada. According to the SCC majority of
2001 it is =
"justified' to force a Frank Paul into conditions of
indoor and outdoor =
homelessness which are KNOWN in advance to have a
Russian-roulette =
probability of causing death because nobody has a duty
to sustain his =
life they say. They added that it would be too costly
to sustain the =
lives of such people which is not credible when we have
the fact that a =
generation earlier homelessness in Canada was a rarity
so the =
administrative system WAS sustaining the lives of
people with the =
"wrong" demographic features (like poor, Indian,
alcoholic, mentally =
ill). Justice was cheapened in 2001 and cheapened to a
shameful and =
shocking degree mindful of what Hitler called his
"useless eaters" =
policy. Although Canada is by Charter/Constitution a
"democratic =
society" perhaps even more democratic measures like the
recall of =
Supreme Court judges for malpractice should be
instituted. If it is =

argued that Frank Paul himself chose the alley, one must examine more =
closely the torturous conditions of indoor facilities called =
=E2=80=9Cshelters=E2=80=9D which are in fact torture chambers. Consider =
Vancouver=E2=80=99s =E2=80=9CAnchor of Hope=E2=80=9D on Cordova Street =
where 100 people sleep on mats a few inches from each other. Airborne =
diseases like TB and influenza are spread rapidly. Half of the cases of =
TB in all of British Columbia are within a few blocks of this =
=E2=80=9CAnchor of Hell=E2=80=9D. What kind of choice did Frank Paul =
have?

Given that cost is an issue though the tragic death of Frank Paul and =
the death and degradation of others by homelessness is given a remedy in =
Gold War. BC will soon be proven as the new South Africa of precious =
metal mining with trillions of dollars in new mineral wealth. The dozen =
or so major Indian national groupings here will start the process of =
uncoupling from Canada. Paid for in minerals, a contest of civilizations =
will result. What we witnessed in 2001 was anathema to civilization. =
CANOPOLIS contestants can suggest ways to solve this social problem and =
many others.

ASK THE EXPERTS!

CHAPTER 10: CATHOLIC CANADIAN CIVILIZATION

I have set before you life and death, blessing and cursing. Choose life =
- Deuteronomy 30:19

Why would Catholic civilization as a "culture of life" not be EAGER to =
lead such a competition of civilizations in BC? The

pages of Catholic =
Catechism (CC) abound in authoritative statements about
the superiority =
of Catholic social-political-economic theory and
practice. Further to =
the CC p 801 "test all things" directive the teaching
masters behind =
those 2,865 paragraphs should be glad of the
opportunity to do so. Many =
thousands of particular services are found under
Canadian constitutional =
"supremacy of God and the rule of law". What if
Parliament were to =
export a Catholic CANOPOLIS to liberated British
Columbia with its =
particular spin on all of those political-legal
services? It would claim =
IHS (In His Service) supremacy over all animal
sacrifices as explained =
in Chapter 7. The sacrifice demanded however is to
sacrifice that which =
is bad and embrace that which is good as I Thess. 5:21
says to "hold =
fast that which is good".

The opening statements of CC invite the entire world to
the table of CC =
questions and answers. Catholic religion includes over
one billion =
adherents and one million clergy (priests, monks,
deacons, nuns et al). =
It includes millions of experts in secular sciences,
arts, law etc. How =
well can it compete with over one billion Muslims
before the "Parliament =
of Man"? Surely Muslims, Hindus, Buddhists and many
other religions =
would also claim adherence to "hold fast that which is
good" as a =
slogan. Can they stand up to the testing/proof which
takes place when =
good, honest questions are put forward?

One has to wonder about the relationship between
Catholic and American =
world outlooks in historical context. Diplomatic
relationships between =

the Papal States/Holy See/Vatican were stopped between 1867 and 1984. =
That is a long time and it was a most serious policy decision. It was =
caused by facts and suspicions over the Lincoln assassination. =
Conspirators met at the boarding house of Mary Surratt of Catholic =
religion and she was executed for her part in the plot. The suspicions =
had to do with how far up the hierarchy this went. Charles Morse of =
Morse code fame and the Canadian Catholic priest Chiniquy reported =
controversial material on what they knew of the plot. Chiniquy may have =
also been the most widely read Canadian author of his day. All these =
names and events can be researched by Internet. But this is the era of =
space colonization and American plans for space colonization compete =
with Catholic plans. The Rock Hunter letter of October 9, 2014 adds an =
up to date note to these historical issues and it is photocopied here. =
It speaks for itself. Chiniquy never revoked small-c catholicism, =
defined as universalism. He might ask today for an articulation of this =
Canadian universality.

Articulation comes in the form of a CANOPOLIS which can migrate =
off-planet without limit in time-space. It is tempting to think of the =
Sto:lo legendary sky-born people as post-flood, post-Noah humans from =
space but that idea might upset Notre Dame University and Salve Regina =
as =E2=80=9CNew Age=E2=80=9D. Yet absence of evidence is not evidence of =
absence. The Bible says nothing about pyramids or saber-toothed tigers =
or giant cave bears. The Bible does not describe the =
=E2=80=9Cgiants=E2=80=9D on the Earth cited in Genesis. Were they =

animals (like the mammoths which co-habited with man),
were they humans =
or were these people mental and psychological giants as
the Sto:lo =
sky-born people are said to be? From early Barbra
Streisand music:

As I was travelling across the sky, this lovely planet
caught my eye,
Being curious I flew close by, and now we=E2=80=99re
caught here til we =
die.

The closing couplet:

Some day we=E2=80=9911 all change into peaceful men,
And we=E2=80=9911 return into the sky

ASK THE EXPERTS!

CHAPTER 11: JUDAIC CANADIAN TESTS

Heaven and earth shall pass away, but my words shall
not pass away - =
Matthew 24:35

This assertion by TJWSHWG is effectively a repetition
of Isaiah 51:6. =
God says the heavens shall pass away like smoke which
is in itself an =
amazing revelation considering that human cosmological
science has only =
recently generated models of how the universe will pass
away. God also =
says in Isaiah that His words shall not pass away.

"Judaism has never called for an unreasoning faith" we
read in the De =
Sola Pool Traditional Jewish Prayer Book. Jews "test
all things'" =
(properly) by sacred tradition. There is no sacred
scripture to an =
unknowing mineral species. The light shines in the
darkness of the rocks =
and the darkness comprehends it not. The light of the
Judahite faith is =
given as a blessing for comprehending persons.

"Salvation is of the =
Jews" Jesus said. Sacred writings or words from
antiquity cannot be =
comprehended without the light of truth which comes
from the Almighty. =
"in Judaism, the flesh became words. Words were the
traditional refuge =
of the Jewish people" (page 54 of "The Talmud and the
Internet by =
Rosen). Rosen also describes a traditional Jewish
custom whereby =
Scriptural messages are written in cake/bread which is
then eaten. This =
hearkens to Ezekial 3:2 and also to John 6:41. The
literal and =
metaphorical relationship of those passages to the
Eucharist or Last =
Supper ritual is of course left to the experts. But
undeniably, TJWSHWG =
declared that unless we abide in Him there is no life
in us and that the =
resurrection of the body for the Israelite faithful as
described in =
Ezekial is by Him.

Scripture trumps tradition and teaching so the metaphor
of three pillars =
requires some elaboration. The second two pillars stand
upon the first. =
They are not equal. The particular form of tradition
changes even while =
meaning may remain constant to the practitioners. No
tradition or =
teaching can be upheld by the faithful if it is in
opposition to =
Scripture and to repeat the passage above, Scripture
can only be =
compehended, sola gracia. In the Red Letters of TJWSHWG,
an Israelite of =
the Tribe of Judah, we read, "Heaven and earth shall
pass away but my =
words shall not pass away" (Matthew 24:35). God's
MEANING in His words =
about Israel shall never pass away. "As the lily dies
only when iits =
scent fouls, so Israel will not die so long as it
executes the commands =

of the Torah and does good deeds" (De Sola Pool, page 879). De Sola Pool =
adds, "The word Torah means teaching" and Rosen says "The Torah is =
celebrated as the living word of God" (page 65). What do =
poiltical-religious experts say about the daily way of life for those =
people who can imagine living in a civilization which is "the best of =
the best"? If 600,000 nomadic people could gather at a mountain several =
thousand years ago and found a new and enlightened nation IHS, why not =
100,000 today in British Columbia en route to an off-planet colony with =
a plan taught to them for the living word of TJWSHWG?.=20

Given the paper of Epstein as cited above on proselytizing Judaism, we =
could say that Zionism is for everyone. Zionism as the establishing of =
an ideal civilization in this world is found in every book of the Bible. =
It is found in every political-religious book. "Ziophobic" people avoid =
this clear and positive meaning of Zionism. A reasoned approach to =
physical and metaphysical phenomena is required by the history of sacred =
traditions of the Judahite people. Reasoning with God is invited in Red =
Letters by the book of Isaiah as even having the power to cure sin. =
Where would we be today if the Jews and Romans of 2,000 years ago in =
Judea had decided to reason with words instead of torture and murder? =
Who are the teaching masters, the magisterium, of Judahite faith? Who =
has exposed the science fraud of Cohen Y chromosome propaganda to use a =
specific example of reasoning at work? Shlomo Sand writes in "When And =
How The Jewish People Was Invented" in accord with Epstein that "varied =

peoples converted to Judaism during the course of
history" and that =
modern Jews "are not at all the descendents of ancient
people who =
inhabiited the Kingdom of Juda during the First and
Second Temple =
Period". This book, published in Haaretz by Ofri Ilani
calls Jewish =
geneology tracings today a "national mythology". That
mythology must =
include the Cohen Y chromosome. Because of the phonetic
similarity of =
the name Cohen to that of the Cohanim priesthood in
Ancient Israel, a =
scientific thesis was put forward that Cohen Y
chromosome constancy =
dated back to that era and that region. But dating a
chromosome back =
3,000 years is questionable at best (because of the
unknown variation in =
mutation rate over those centuries) and even if
validated it proves =
nothing. Chromosomes do not have surnames in double
helix chemistry. The =
original family name bearing this chromosome is not
known. Dogmatic =
declarations about region of origin are even more
speculative. "Middle =
East" is a huge region which goes even beyond Greater
Israel (Nile to =
Euphrates). Ancient people were also well travelled as
the silk roads =
(plural) through Afghanistan and Pakistan prove. Do a
search on =
Karakoram Highway, the 8th wonder of the world. The
Cohen Y chromosome =
even claims a historical occurrence in the Lamba tribe
of southern =
Africa. It is generally accepted that the surname Cohen
and all =
variations like Kahan, Cohn, Cohen, Kaplan and about 50
others are =
derived from the name Kaganovitch/Kagan which
originated between the =
Black and Caspian seas. In accord with Shlomo Sand's
position that many =
Jews today are "for the most part descendents of pagans

who converted to =
Judaism" the pagan name Kaganovitch seems more likely to have a =
Japhethite history rather than Shemite/Semite and it was "modernized" to =
Kahan which is the phonetic root of all the later variants. Constancy of =
the chromosome is easily achieved by the expulsion or elimination of =
illegitimate male children and by having no male adoptions. Kagans and =
others converted to Judaism during one of the waves of proselytizing as =
discussed by Epstein., in this case the 7th to 11th centuries AD. =
Consider again the role of silk roads as names wander far and wide with =
their owners. We read on the wiki/Khan_(title) that Kagan is also a =
title which means "sovereign or military ruler" and that Ghenghis Khan =
is a famous example of this title. "His title was Khagan ('Khan of =
Khans', see below, but is oftened shortened to Khan".=20

Some, like Professor Shlomo Sand may argue that Jewish civilization is =
"invented" or created but that is not derogatory in any way. On the =
contrary it is a stroke of genius which recognizes facts in the =
historical record. There is almost no record, Biblical or secular, which =
describes what the Israelites did over 400 years in Egypt before the =
Exodus circa 1450 BC. Hebrew language can only be traced back to circa =
1,000 BC so we do not even have a record of the language spoken by =
Jacob/Israel or Moses. Creativity is not a fault or vice. How could the =
Israelites not be culturally creative as Jacob's small family grew to a =
nation of 600,000 subordinated to Egyptian cultural masters, under the =
Babylonian captivity and then Roman occupation? Each

would lead to =
intermarriage with adversarial cultures and thus
biological as well as =
cultural transformation. We read in "The Standard
Jewish Encyclopedia" =
(1966, page 594) that "The Edomites were conquered by
John Hyrcanus who =
forcibly converted them to Judaism and from then on
they constituted =
part of the Jewish people, Herod being one of their
descendents". The =
Israellites were people of law but all nations who have
ever inhabited =
Earth are populated by people of law. No society has
ever existed here =
in a state of chaos which is what some seem to be
advocating when they =
talk about "The Singularity" of transhumanism as an
imminent =
social-political event. That is folly. The question
then is what law =
code applicable to the time and place of this space era
might a =
Neo-Judaic civilization generate or invent. Not one jot
or tittle of The =
Law changes but the spirit of the law is adaptive. Good,
healthful =
dieting never changes as a principle of law. The
particulars of diet and =
dining etiquette do change. Some traditions are deemed
sacred and are =
resistant to change but they do change in practice
while staying =
constant in principle.=20

What blessings will British Columbian cultural
inventions bring the =
world? The Cold War was won by the test of gates. Open
the gates or =
borders between nations and see which way the
population moves. Who will =
move into the liberated nations of a free and
balkanized British =
Columbia? What designs for future civilization and
future sapiens will =
originate with the present day nations whose
colonialist ancestors came =

here in the 1700s and 1800s? Gold War explains how Russia, United =
States, Great Britain, Spain and Canada were major rivals. Canada won =
the colonialism contest for BC with the illegal colonialist annexation =
of this region in 1871. But this was not a just or legal victory. Canada =
has no claim over the natural resources of BC from justice, military =
conquest or any other rationale. What do the political parties of Canada =
as represented in Parliament say to this in Question Period? What do the =
Conservative, Liberal, Green and New Democratic parties say? What does =
the Bloc Quebecois party say? What does BQ say to a Bloc Indian Party =
(BIP) in BC? Such a party could easily be registered by UBCIC (Union of =
BC Indian Chiefs) and the sea to sea to sea AFN (Assembly of First =
Nations). It can be discussed as a matter of national importance without =
runniing in a single election. Does BQ accept its platform of UN =
membership for BC First Nations? Does BQ accept a generalization of that =
UN membership to the northern Cree or southern Iroquois of Quebec?

Modern =E2=80=9CIsrael=E2=80=9D appears to be a conglomerate of revived =
Edomite, Midian, Hittite, Canaanite and other micro-nations from the =
past of the Arabian Peninsula region (=E2=80=9CLevant=E2=80=9D). How =
else can one explain Golda Meier=E2=80=99s lament about the 1/3 Atheists =
in her flock? Moses would have immediately killed such people amongst =
his flock.
The resurrection referred to in Ezekial and Daniel which appears to have =
impacted Greco-Roman metaphysical philosophy can be collectively and =
metaphorically applied to a resurrected Israellite

CANOPOLIS of 100,000. =
Or should that be 100,000 x 12 with a CANOPOLIS for
each tribe? Since we =
know so little about the ancient civilizations of Jacob
(Israel) and his =
twin brother, Esau (Edom) how can we today match
latter-day Israel with =
latter-day Edom? What kind of civilization would law
and justice =
scholars describe today for each according to the
ideals of each twin? =
Apply that also to the chapter below on Chinese
Canadian Civilization.
Historically there are precedents for electing kings.
Both New Israel =
and New Edom might elect their =E2=80=9CKing of the
Jews=E2=80=9D as a =
modern Herod.

Again, from Leonard Cohen and The Future:

It=E2=80=99s once for the Devil and it=E2=80=99s once
for Christ,
But the Boss don=E2=80=99t like these dizzy heights,
We=E2=80=99re busted in the blinding lights,
Of closing time.

ASK THE EXPERTS!

CHAPTER 12: MUSLIM CANADIAN CIVILIZATION

And the land which I gave to Abraham and Isaac, I will
give to you and =
your seed - Genesis 35:12

Rushdie found himself under a fatwa (religion-based
death threat) for =
publishing his book about Koran under the title Satanic
Verses. But we =
use an expression like THE Koran without thinking what
a small and =
important word means - THE. Any Koran is only a set of
markings on paper =
or other medium unless it is interpreted There may be
as many =

interpretations as there are readers. Whose is correct? Whose is =
satanic? If a code of law is generated from A Koran, whose code is to be =
accepted as the foundation for a Muslim civilization in BC? Koran =
originated with an Arab commander-in-chief, Mohammed Abdullah whose =
empire is the most successful the world has ever seen without leaving =
home, the Mecca-Medina region. His words on religion pertain to =
truncated references on about only 25 Biblical personages out of the =
hundreds in a Bible. They are also sayings which were independently =
understood by many others with the name of Mohammed which was common =
even then. These ideas like the repudiation of the Holy Trinity were =
circulated by millions of people in the Middle East and Mediterranean =
region. It took 25 years or so after the death of Mohammed Abdulladh for =
Caliph Bakr to gather the beliefs into a single book, called Koran. That =
was written in Classical Arabic so the problem of multiple =
interpretations is complicated further. Few people today understand =
Classical Arabic.

Muslim foundations in Koran and associated law (sometimes called Sharia) =
do however have some constancies like rejection of Trinitarian teaching =
and another important one is the rejection of the Red Letter words of =
the Bible on inheritance law pertaining to the descendents of Abraham. =
In Genesis 15:18 we find these Red Letter words identifying a =
super-nation between the Nile and Euphrates rivers. In Genesis18:18 God =
says all the persons of the earth shall be blessed in Abraham and his =
super-nation but in Genesis 35:12 God says with perfect

clarity that the =
land which was given to Abraham and then his son Isaac is passed on =
further to Israel, son of Isaac and in Israel all the people of the =
earth shall be blessed (Genesis 28:14). That also seems to explain the =
Koranic truncation of Biblical messages as cited above. Muslim =
civilization cannot accept the Biblical God whose central inheritance in =
the Middle East names Israel as having rightful title to all that is =
called Saudi Arabia today, including Mecca and Medina. That Mecca-Medina =
region is immediately southward of modern Jordan which is Biblical Edom. =
It was called Midian and Moses was quite familiar with it as the =
territory of his distant cousins. Ottawa politicians may prefer to avoid =
the contentious issues of religion but they cannot be avoided if anyone =
is to understand the war raging from North Africa to Afghanistan today =
and its result at home in a Vancouver Sun headline like that of October =
23, 2014, "Terror Rocks The Nation's Capital". History and ideology =
(beliefs) underlie such events.

Multiculturalism as a political platform however, can still take a =
positive stance. The same test applies to all cultures in Canada =
equally. Point by point __________ is a good feature to incorporate into =
a model Muslim civilization in BC because ____________. If Arab-based =
(Mecca-based) civilization is the best of the best, prove it. Prove it =
here in Canada, peacefully. Prove that the Muslim repudiation of the God =
of the Bible is correct and that all nations shall be blessed in it more =
than Israel. BC has room for many future cities. It is twice the area of =

Japan. When the gates are open will migrating people of
the world flock =
into a Muslim city, a Catholic city, a Buddhist city, a
_______ city?

It only requires Muslim CANOPOLIS contestants to
complete the sentence =
_____________ is a good feature of a Muslim CANOPOLIS
because =
_____________________ in accordance with the definition of =
=E2=80=9Cgood=E2=80=9D in Koran 75:13, =E2=80=9CThe =
Resurrection=E2=80=9D which says, =E2=80=9CThen man
will be told what he =
had sent ahead (of good) and what he had left
behind=E2=80=9D. Will the =
Muslim CANOPOLIS be the =E2=80=9Cbest of the
best=E2=80=9D among scores =
or perhaps hundreds of future reservations in Canada?
Will it be the =
model of =E2=80=9Cpeace, order and good
government=E2=80=9D? Will the =
American CANOPOLIS declare that =E2=80=9CWhen America
ceased to be good =
it ceased to be great .... until it discovered the
goodness of =
Islam=E2=80=9D? Does the Muslim CANOPOLIS Constitution
begin with, =
=E2=80=9CWhereas Muslim CANOPOLIS is founded upon
principles that =
recognize the supremacy of Allah
                              =E2=80=9D?
____

ASK THE EXPERTS!

CHAPTER 13: CHINESE CANADIAN CIVILIZATION

There is something formed of chaos,
Born before heaven and earth,
Silent and void, it is not renewed.
It goes on forever without failing.

- Tao Te Ching

 What color should be used for the words above from the
Tao Te Ching? =
Why? In China, red is the color of celebration, the
color of good news =

which is Gospel news. China towns are popular in Canada. Why not a China =
City of 100,000? And what ideology/religion/belief system should it use =
for the CANOPOLIS Constitution? Consider the twins, Happy Nappy Ho of =
the CIA (Chinese Intelligence Agency) and Nappy Happy Ho of the CIA =
(Canadian Intelligence Agency) ... or is it vice-versa? Tell us a Tale =
Of Two Chinese cities for the CANOPOLIS constitutional contest. China is =
a multireligious country and in that sense it is multicultural. =
Xinjiang, the largest province in area adjoins Pakistan and links to =
Gilgit Province in Pakistan by the Karakorum Highway which is one of the =
wonders of the modern world. Xinjiang religion is mostly Muslim. The =
highest Karakorum pass is above most clouds at three miles. Fine ice =
crystals fall instead of rain. BC=E2=80=99s highest mountain (Robson) is =
only about two miles above sea level. The tree line in BC is at one =
mile. Above that we look up to our mountains and see bare rock.=20

China has a historic benefit when it comes to thinking about Moon =
civilization because millions of people still live in mountain caves. =
Not only is there a problem of radiation from space for those living on =
the Moon but there is also a problem of rocks in all sizes falling from =
the sky since it contains almost no atmosphere to vaporize even the =
smallest stone. One bean-sized rock could be deadly. A survey of Chinese =
troglodyte culture by Nappy and Nappy would be a good start. For =
example, south exposure would probably be preferred in China and that =
means a sunny location on the Moon is best. Darker and cooler places are =

found when colonists tunnel into rock. There are health problems =
associated with mineral content as is the case for asbestos-family =
minerals and minerals which are highly radioactive. Mental health =
problems are also linked to claustrophobia and excessive darkness as =
well as poor air circulation (stale air).

What of Chinese CANOPOLIS religion? The CIA is fully aware that Xinjiang =
is almost the only troubled region in China at the time of this writing =
and the Muslim provinces bordering India and Pakistan are almost the =
only troubled region for India where the world=E2=80=99s biggest =
infantry face-off exists (comparable to Eastern-Western European =
face-offs during World War 2 and Cold War). The CIA is not fooled into =
thinking that the Muslim religion has nothing to do with this though =
propagandizing media in general would have us believe that the global =
terrorism epidemic is brought to us by people who =E2=80=9Cjust happen =
to be Muslims=E2=80=9D. The CANOPOLIS Contest requires that the =
connection between beliefs and practices is made clear.

Nappy Happy Ho can text in the winning CANOPOLIS essay along with a new =
Canadian flag with the red removed ... or will it be Happy Nappy Ho =
whose flag has the white removed?

CHAPTER 14: THE INEFFABLE CANADIAN=20

I am the root and the offspring of David, and the bright and morning =
star - Revelation 22:16

The late, great psychiatrist K Dabrowski was a faculty member at the =
University of Alberta. His theory of "positive

disintegration" as he =
called it put forward the idea that social and
psychological =
disintegration often precedes a positive re-integration
for the better. =
This is in keeping with the words of TJWSHWG that
unless a seed falls to =
the ground it cannot grow. The uncoupling of BC from
Canada is firstly a =
disintegration of Canada but the resulting
reintegration will take =
Canada forward ad astra. This is the fruition of
decades of large scale =
immigration and multiculturalism and the nationwide
cure of xenophobia. =
Imagine BC with double the population of Japan. With
twice the area of =
Japan and a friendly competition between the dozen or
so major First =
Nation groupings for personnel resources, a population
in the hundreds =
of millions is sustainable, especially as minerals and
power are =
exported back to BC from colonies on Moon, Mars and
beyond. To give an =
idea of the magnitude of these resources, consider what
Yeomans writes =
in Chapter 7 of his "Near-Earth Objects" book. Chapter
7 is titled =
:Nature's Natural Resources and the Human Exploration
of our Solar =
System". He notes that even a lower grade and not so
large rocky =
asteroid may contain trillions of dollars worth of
metals. There are =
thousands of these asteroids on the Moon.=20

Positive reintegration of BC as the sovereign and
independent entity it =
legally has been all along will allow Canada to spell
out its model of =
Canadian ideals and submit them to lawful First Nation
BC authorities. =
After so many years of multiculturalism, the MPs and
Senators of Ottawa =
must have clear ideas about which features of those
various cultures are =

the best of the best contrasted with those which are regressive and =
harmful. Positive disintegration does not mean termination or =
extermination. Faith without works is dead. That popular statement is =
derived from the catechism of all catechisms, the Bible. In CC p 170 we =
read "The believer's act (of faith) does not terminate in the =
propositions but in the realities (which they express)". What is the =
Canadian reality?

Shallow political-judicial jingoisms and slogans do not constitute =
integrity. Political-judicial actors on stage can skillfully be imitated =
by Hollywood or Bollywood actors. The same can be said for simulations =
of religiosity, piety and holiness. Movies like Oh God, Almighty Bruce, =
Oh My God (Bollywood), Angels and Demons, Apparitions (BBC) and others =
prove this so well. Angels and Demons (Ron Howard producer) presents the =
circumstance of an impostor pope putting himself forward as the King of =
Rome on the Throne of Christ which is not in itself such an extreme =
possibility. The Roman Catholic religion has formally identified some =
two dozen such impostors over the past 2,000 years. What then =
differentiates true Romanist civilization from an impostor?

A Judahite core of civilization rose up, Phoenix-like from the ashen =
circumstances of the torture and murder of Jesus Christ. TJWSHWG makes =
the point by apologetics that to create this as a fiction or fable which =
people will then immediately adhere to even at the cost of their lives =
is almost impossible. Where are the "creative writers" today to show how =

it could have been done? Even the imaginative BBC
cannot do this. The =
ecclesiastical history of the Bible gives some numbers.
There were 120 =
of the faithful at the beginning of Acts who probably
studied with Jesus =
Christ, the Torah personified post-resurrection and
pre-ascencion and =
subsequently Acts presents repeated reference to
"thousands" of new =
adherents There were 500+ in a "brotherhood" who
claimed to have =
witnessed the miracle of all miracles, the resurrection
of TJWSHWG. =
These were the hundreds and the thousands of Jews who
did not find the =
perfect offering of Jesus to be a stumbling block and
by cruel irony of =
history their descendants today are denied right of
return to Israel =
while atheists in large numbers are admitted. But the
superiority of =
this Judahite civilization today can become that p 170
reality in BC.

Canadian nationalism is not so shallow to consist of
lines on a map. =
Look at the geopolitical maps of history. The change in
border =
boundaries is enormous. Many nations have disappeared
by name. New =
nations have arisen. The UN has only about 200 members.
But the number =
of national groupings who could be members is in the
thousands. Where is =
the Basque nation in the UN General Assembly? Ireland,
once part of UK =
has a seat. Where is the UN delegate of Scotland? Will
nations in space =
be offshoots of nations on this planet or will they
create new national =
entities? Canadianism is idealism in search of
actualization. BC, =
liberated from a fraudulent natural resource grab by
the greedy of =
Ottawa in 1871 can give Canadianism that reality.=20

The New Canada will truly be a DOMAIN and in that sense
merits a new =
name as so many nations have now renamed themselves.
One possibility is =
The Domain of Canada. This denotes the rebirth of a =
spiritually/ideologically born-again Canada which
fairly embraces all =
cultures equally in just competition without the
current pathetically =
inadequate Charter s15 interpretation that we get from
=E2=80=9CNew =
World Order=E2=80=9D sycophants in the political-
judicial system. Such =
people flee like cockroaches when the light of good,
honest questions =
impinges on their pathetic exercises in casuistry
applied to the =
hundreds of religions and the hundreds of sexual
orientations in this =
world. They are not all equal in fact but they are
equally entitled to =
compete. The New Canadian is still as ineffable as the
(somewhat =
tongue-in-cheek) CIA of Chapter 13 and its
=E2=80=9Ccosmological top =
secret=E2=80=9D projects. By the time Japan, Russia et
al are building =
their Moon colonies which is expected to be 2030, the
New Canadian will =
emerge from the darkness of the current political-
judicial system. This =
one-party system was called NDP (NoDamnedPrinciples) or
=E2=80=9CParty =
of the Trough=E2=80=9D in Gold War. Arguably Deputy
Prime Minister =
Nielsen understated when he called Parliament a den of
liars and FLQ =
leader Vallieres likewise understated when he wrote
=E2=80=9CWhite =
Niggers=E2=80=9D. Future Canada is much brighter than
those writings =
convey.

ASK THE EXPERTS!

CHAPTER 15: TRUE LOVE AND CANADIAN PARLIAMENTARY
CATECHISM

Love God with all your heart and soul and mind and
strength - Mark 12:29

JW Woodside's Foreward to the Divine services Book For
The Canadian =
Armed Forces (1950) says "This book is designed to meet
the religious =
needs of the men and women in the various branches of
the Forces". =
Today, a multicultural/multireligious Canada must face
the reality that =
all religions have the constitutional right to equality
(Charter section =
15) which means each has the equal right to prove that
its WAY OF LIFE =
is "the best of the best". It does not mean that all
religions are =
inherently equal. When God is defined as =E2=80=9Cthe
best of the =
best=E2=80=9D and the source of all blessings who can
confer them on any =
of us, even the Atheist can accept the Mark 12:29
citation.

The Canadian political-judicial system has no
jurisdiction over natural =
resources in British Columbia. It is ultra vires.
Personnel or human =
resources are another matter. As First Nations of BC
take their places =
in the UN General Assembly over the next century,
leases like the =
now-expired Hong Kong lease can be negotiated between
these personnel, =
their MP and Senate representatives, and Canada. The
new immigration =
policy of BC will be in First Nation hands, empowered
by new-found =
precious metal discoveries in the trillions of dollars
as "Gold War" =
predicts. Religion is merely an act which Hollywood,
Bollywood and BBC =
actors simulate with ease unless it is translated into
a comprehensive =
way of life, 24/7. Canada must concede that the Indian
people of BC have =

never given up their natural resource rights. It is not a matter of =
"giving them back". They never belonged to Canada. What will =
concentrated populations of human resources nested within BC Indian =
nations yield? Which is "the best of the best"?

A $5,000 advance on royalties for CCCC (Catholic Catechism Critique =
Corrected) was offered in Catholic Catechism Critique (Friesen) and =
NEWTOWN (Kindle).

This offer is in accord with the GODBOT presentation above. GODBOT is =
first a grammarian. If experts in religious doctrine or teaching mastery =
at Catholic and Protestant universities in particular are not eager to =
come forward to the light of day before billions of people now =
text-machine connected and correct what some will see as a heresy, why =
not? Do they not understand the Golden Rule? I correct you and you =
correct me. If they are by contrast not willing to come forward and =
proclaim it a breakthrough in religious analysis and understanding, why =
not? The Israelite Magisterium and Torah defined as sacred teaching =
tradition (De Sola Pool) calls for us to "love good and hate evil" and =
thus we, like King David "hate those who hate Thee (God) with a perfect =
hatred". Who is the God of the Canadian Constitution? "Whereas Canada is =
founded upon the supremacy of God ____________"? God is love says the =
Gospel of John. But we have an expression in English vernacular: TRUE =
LOVE. Does Parliament love evil? The United Nations is little more than =
a debating club for rich and powerful despots, many being the =
concentrated evil of humankind (although Indian nation

entry will have =
symbolic value pertaining to recognition of autonomy).
Is Parliament =
mostly likewise ... a debating club for men/women/other
driven by ego =
and greed? Does it have the expertise to welcome a
political-religious =
catechism of good, honest questions and good, honest
answers? Can it =
spell out on the blank screens of GODBOT, a computer in
humanoid form, =
that which is both good and true? Or do we say that
Parliament loves =
evil and hates good which seems to be the theme of the
perversely bad =
BBC series "Misfits"? Can the English Parliament even
analyze "Misfits" =
without groveling before the twisted English deity of
political =
correctness? Can they "talk about what the English are
not supposed to =
talk about" or do we say the modern English
parliamentarian is too much =
the liar and coward to do so? Are the Red Letter words
of Revelation =
21:8 a description of the future King Charles as head
of the Church of =
England? Obviously TJWSHWG did not come to save us from
the first death =
but those who commit themselves to lies rather than Him
are not saved =
from the second death we read in Rev 21:8. "Every time
I look into the =
Holy Book I want to tremble" sings Canadian folk singer
Ann Murray. If =
King Charles assisted by all of his bishops and
parliamentarians cannot =
tell BBC or GODBOT the difference between true love and
false love, can =
the Canadian Parliament help him out? "Misfits" seems
designed by those =
who love twisted perversity, sexually and otherwise.
The English ship of =
state is lost at sea. Canada's Parliament can do better
than that and =
guide them to safe harbor.

ASK THE EXPERTS!

CLOSING

And many false prophets shall arise, and deceive many -
Matthew 24:11

What are the words of the prophets? Sometimes they are written on the =
subway walls as Simon and Garfunkel say. Sometimes they are written on =
the hard drives and thumb drives of GODBOT teaching machines. How would =
a Xulon Press God Tube interview with GODBOT at Notre Dame's God Quad =
play out? What questions about Catholic Catechism would the Xulon =
interviewer as expert representative ask GODBOT and the Notre Dame =
professors? What questions would self-proclaimed religion experts =
pronounce anathema or heretical even though they are important matters =
of life and death in the public domain? An Internet search on religious =
honorifics and titles reveals an astonishing plethora of =
self-aggrandizing vanities. If this self-proclaimed holiness, divinity, =
piety and revered status is more than vanity they will be eager to come =
forward and prove their expertise about how we should live on this =
planet and beyond. Otherwise, the Biblical assertion that there is none =
righteous, no not one, with related passages stand firm. The world is =
awash in religious fraud. The Catholic Catechism paragraph 801 testing =
of all things is easily applied to Catholic catechizers. Deceivers who =
run away at Notre Dame and elsewhere prove who they serve by such =
testing.

Some of these moral matters are technologically

disguised. Space age =
technologies can save many lives. Does "Thou shalt not kill" ring the =
proverbial bell? Modern technology can export transportation systems =
which rarely take a human life. The city core of Vancouver on the other =
hand takes about 30 lives per year in vehicular accidents. The =
post-traumatic disorders afflicted upon family, friends and even police =
and other first responders may not heal in a life time. Do the religion =
experts want sclerotic, life-destroying transportation technology =
exported to the Canadian Moon? Consider the "flying train" of Robert =
Goddard, dubbed the progenitor of American rocket science. It was he who =
first proposed what is today called the hyperloop in California, about =
to be built by Hyperloop Transportation Technology Inc. and not =
robophobe billionaire, Elon Musk despite what he might claim in bragging =
rights. Goddard patented the idea of a vacuum or near-vacuum tube with a =
train which could attain up to space speeds. It is about to be tested in =
California by Hyperloop Transportation Technology Inc which has also =
inked a deal with land owners for the track.

Bombardier Canada technologies on the Moon will use Goddard ideas which =
hybridize the plane and the train. The magnetic levitation train or =
mag-lev is in effect a plane-train combination. It is a flying train. On =
the Moon it needs no vacuum tube. Because of the low gravity as well, =
flying trains could be propelled from the Moon into space perhaps with =
mountains like the Mountain of Eternal Light as launch ramps. Bombardier =
which is sometimes government subsidized, is Canada's leading =

transportation technology expert. The company describes itself as NUMBER =
ONE GLOBALLY in the manufacture and sale of trains and planes in =
combination. It could even create the CANOPOLIS transportation system =
here in BC, first on paper. Since Bombardier receives government =
funding, it would be appropriate for Parliament to ask it for plans to a =
CANOPOLIS transportation system which would meet the criteria of "little =
or no pollution" and "few, if any, fatalities". Integrated technologies =
would range from moving sidewalks to sky trains (like the one operating =
since 1986 with an almost perfect safety record) to interplanetary =
plane-train hybrids.

Words have to be put into practice. The words of the Bible in and of =
themselves have no meaning. They are only atoms and molecules fashioned =
into ink, computer screen markings and so on as stated repeatedly in =
earlier chapters. GODBOT is a machine tabula rasa until =
political-religious experts revive the catechism genre of literature and =
prove otherwise. BC can send a GODBOT to Library of Parliament to serve =
as chief librarian. Perhaps it will be built by lely.com or its =
westcoastrobotics.com branch in BC as an "astronaut" model. It will walk =
and talk like ASIMO or NAO. This will be a $6,000,000 humanoid. That is =
a fair price tag. When will it be delivered?

ASK THE EXPERTS!

Rock Hunter
Sto:lo Nation, British Columbia, 2016

EXCURSUS

And he that hateth his life in this world shall keep it unto life =
eternal - John 12:25

What if we use this emphasis: He that hateth his life in THIS world =
___________? Catholic Catechism says in paragraph 2,852 that "the whole =
world is in the power of the evil one". Does that not mean both =
institutions of church and state? Does that mean we must export an =
equally evil model of the civilization which is "in this world" =
off-planet? If religious people at Notre Dame, the Curia in Rome and =
among the thousands of Xulon and Friesen contributors are not always "in =
the power of the evil one" should they not be EAGER to come forward and =
tell the world about their shining city on a hill, their CANOPOLIS, =
worthy of export to Moon, Mars and beyond? If life in THIS world is =
justifiably hated, emigrate to another world.

What should it be like? ASK THE EXPERTS! Those experts in academia who =
cannot use first person Socratic dialogue (or its eastern equivalent) to =
engage GODBOT in the many necessary questions are not truly learned =
people. They are just pinheads. What questions should three wise men of =
the west like the =E2=80=9Cthree amigos=E2=80=9D, Trump, Ventura and =
Black ask GODBOT? How would they differ from the questions of three wise =
men of the east who went to Judea to meet =E2=80=9CThe King of the =
Jews=E2=80=9D?

The GODBOT script above was written with the intention of being as =
objective as the rain which falls on the just and the

unjust concerning =
scientific and technological possibilities. But this in
no way condones =
moral or cultural relativity or "new age" doctrine
defined by =
quasi-religious ideology which tries to turn fiction
and superstition =
into fact as a foundation for choices in life.This
impartial objectivity =
was not always adhered to but the GODBOT writing stance
was a way of =
inviting experts from all fields to make their
contributions toward =
Future Canada. This Excursus is an advocacy of
accepting BIBLICAL TRUTH =
as a foundation for all belief and thus non-believers
are fairly warned =
of the material which follows. BIBLICAL TRUTH can only
be comprehended =
Sola Gracia. Only guided by the Holy Spirit of God,
meaning Absolute =
Truth can the Bible be understood. This reality
generalizes. Only if we =
are guided by TRUTH will be able to understand ANY
writing or even a =
non-writing, a blank page. Only guided by TRUTH can we
understand any =
communication, including the information communicated
by nature. The =
following reasoning is deliberately circular. The Bible
is the inerrant =
word of God because the inerrant word of God is the
Bible.

The writer's belief system is solidly founded upon the
Trinitarian =
Apostles' Creed. No apology is made for that. This
Creed is the =
monotheistic light of Judaism carried forward by the
nation of Judah =
under Roman occupation. The Old Testament is not merely
a book (or =
collection of books) about God. It is a book by God.
God is speaking to =
man throughout this book. Those words are His Red
Letter words. Black =
letter words are commentary, analysis, reflection and

so on as they =
pertain to what God is saying. Witnesses, reporters,
writers are the =
people who have a secondary role to this Authorship.
Expert Bible =
scholars can comment on HOW those Red Letter words are
expressed. Two =
sensory modalities only are mentioned in the Bible -
sight and sound =
(voice) with touch being a rare exception (Thomas
touched the wound of =
Jesus). God is seen and heard. The language spoken by
God must have been =
understandable to recipients who spoke different
languages. The =
Hebrew-Eberic languages changed greatly over hundreds
and thousands of =
years. Otherwise, no clarification of God's language is
given in the =
Bible. What language was used in the early sections of
Genesis which =
were long before any Hebrew language? What language did
God use to speak =
to Adam and Eve? How does the Hebrew which He
presumably spoke to =
Jacob/Israel or Moses compare to the Hebrew used in
Israel today? What =
language did Jesus speak in the Gospels? Did He speak
to the learned =
religious leaders using the Hebrew of the day or the
Hebrew of =
Jacob/Israel or the Hebrew of Moses? Did He speak to
the crowds in =
Aramaic and Romans like Pilate in Latin? What is the
meaning of God's =
multilingual miracle in Chapter 2 of Acts,
communicating to the devout =
Jews out of every nation under heaven?

The Bible, Sola Gracia can only be understood as a
series of =
questionable statements. Did TJWSHWG ever turn away a
good, honest =
question? Since God does not want us to be deceived by
impostors, surely =
He wants us to ask lots of good, honest questions to
the catechizers of =

all religions and thus find out who the wolves in sheep=E2=80=99s' =
clothing are. For example, when we read Koran, 2:85-87 "Remember We gave =
Moses the Book and sent after him many an apostle; and to Jesus, son of =
Mary, We gave clear evidence of the truth". Who =3D "We" in this =
passage? Who =3D "I" in Chapter 75 which is titled "The Resurrection"? =
It is not Allah because this unnamed =E2=80=9CI=E2=80=9D is said in that =
chapter to be speaking in the name of Allah. And thus "When will the Day =
of Resurrection be?" (75:6) and who will define the =
=E2=80=9Cgood=E2=80=9D deeds of 75:13 which speak for a favorable =
resurrection? Since Classical Arabic is read by very few today, which of =
these readers decides what the words We and I mean in this context or =
what anything in Koran means? Or does that "Numero Uno" position among =
readers falls to someone today who is not familiar with Classical =
Arabic? Who constitutes the =E2=80=9CMagisterium=E2=80=9D of Islam? =
Would that seniormost position of reader/interpreter also mean the =
reader is most senior to serve as WRITER of the GODBOT C program? Space =
is left here for a C program as the GOBDOT pages in RAM and hard drive =
are blank. You and the experts must write them. Catechizing wolves of =
all belief systems in sheep=E2=80=99s clothing will run away from the =
truth which shines from good, honest questions. They are the liars =
and/or cowards of Revelation 21:8 whose eternity after the second death =
is surely hellish if they are committed to the lies. Is there any =
so-called Christian teaching institution which can describe a Christian =
CANOPOLIS compared to a Muslim CANOPOLIS or shall we say that =

today=E2=80=99s religious teaching institutions are frauds against both =
God and man?

The medium is not the message. Many questions may be asked about the =
medium for Red Letter words. A few details are given in the Bible. =
Nature may be cited as a medium (for example the whirlwind by which God =
spoke to Job) and natural phenomena, often dramatic, like lightning and =
great storms and fire, may accompany the Red Letter words. Are these not =
part of the language of God - a non-verbal language? What are the limits =
on this language of performance? Given that God is all-powerful, there =
is no theoretical limit. God can use GODBOT as a medium IHS (In His =
Service).

We are all familiar with the saying, "an act of God". All acts must be =
either directly or indirectly acts of God since God is all powerful. =
What do the experts in religion and theology say about evil acts? What =
do we read in Genesis 3:22 and Isaiah 45:7? Since God=E2=80=99s power is =
immeasurably above ours, there are times when He says, Do as I say and =
not as I do. Evil as well as good are His responsibility. There is no =
instance in the Bible of Red Letter words which tell humans to =
perpetrate evil. What do the experts say of the cruelty in nature? Is it =
good or evil or neither? A child's hymn says: "This is my Father's world =
... He speaks to me everywhere". Is every act or expression in nature a =
Red Letter expression? Canadian folksinger Gordon Lightfoot sings "Does =
anyone know where the love of God goes?" ("The Wreck of the Edmund =
Fitzgerald"). And what do we read in Matthew 27:46?

"Eli, Eli, lama =
sabachthani?" God has dual responsibility for good and
evil but man is =
directed only to do good. CANOPOLIS and GODBOT are
about peace, order =
and good government.

Red Letters of the Bible advocate only the expression
of good over evil =
and some will say this is utopianism. But God never
says, Do good only =
in limited places and at limited times. The Kingdom of
Heaven is =
advocated as a ideal which is to be turned into a
reality on this planet =
24/7. That ideal is pre-eminently why Jews and Romans
colluded in =
deicide 2,000 years ago. The Roman emperor was self-
deified and the Jews =
feared that they would be ruthlessly persecuted if they
announced that =
they must serve God rather than man as is stated in
Acts. Yet this is =
the Zionist ideal, found in every book where God speaks
to His Chosen =
People. Their beliefs were taught to the entire world
so Zionism became =
a global ideal. Babies born in Canada now can expect to
see colonies on =
Moon and Mars when they are adults. What kind of
CANOPOLIS will Canada =
export off-planet as the reality of this global ideal?

Russia is red, dilly dilly;
England is green.
We've got the Moon, dilly dilly;
They've got the Queen.

The Bible never says to reject the natural laws. It
advocates REASONING =
and PROOF/TESTING. Let us reason together ______ What
do we call =
narrow-minded people stuck in blind religious dogmas
(or worse, dogmas =
which are known to be false)? We call them dogmatic
bigots. What do we =
call academics who reject the miracles of Intelligent

Design and =
Creation/Creative Science as presented in the Bible while accepting the =
miracles of quantum teleportation and bilocation? They too are dogmatic =
bigots. On the level of explanation or theory neither Biblical miracles =
nor laboratory quantum miracles =E2=80=9Cmake sense=E2=80=9D because our =
minds are too limited to grasp the explanation. The lead actor in the =
movie, =E2=80=9CThe Life of Pi=E2=80=9D is a Hindu who studies world =
religions. Pi says the substitutionary atonement miracle whereby the =
blood of Jesus pays for our sins =E2=80=9Cmakes no sense at =
all=E2=80=9D. Neither does quantum teleportation make sense to any =
physicist. In both cases the facts are within our grasp. What do we say =
of so-called Christians who reject good, honest questions and answers in =
all manner of catechisms? Chillingly the flock is small and straight is =
the gate, narrow is the way and few there be that find it. Therefore, it =
is a miracle that there are those few who love truth, who are wholly =
dedicated to truth, who are invited to seek and do find this truth.=20

It is irrefutable that the Holy Book declares truth to be of two kinds: =
natural and super-natural. What then do we say of BC's tourism slogan - =
"Super, Natural, BC"? BC WILL balkanize over this century. Canada will =
accept that the 1871 colonialist seizure was an act of theft. Canada =
will apologize to the First Nations of BC for ongoing genocide of those =
with demographics like Frank Paul (poor/Indian/mentally ill) which =
became a nation-wide attack on the poor of all ethnicities. As a result =
of GODBOT's never-ending Question Period (perhaps with

a 5-13 robot =
ensconced at the Library of Parliament) Canada will
enter the era of =
space colonization and BC will lead Canada after it is
liberated from =
Ottawa colonialism. The seed which falls to the ground
will become the =
"Catechism Of The Future History Of New Canada"
according to a =
CANOPOLIS definition of civilization and of Canadian.
These are the =
Canadians who will travel to the Moon and some will
live there =
indefinitely. They will regard themselves as Moonlings.
They will be our

FUTURE SAPIENS.

REFERENCES

Asimov, Isaac. Asimov's Guide To The Bible: The Old
Testament, Avon =
Books, 1968

Axworthy, Thomas S. and Trudeau, Pierre Elliott (Eds).
Towards A Just =
Society: The Trudeau Years, Viking, 1990

Catechism of the Catholic Church. Pope John Paul II
(Karol Josef =
Wojtyla) edition, The Liturgical Press, 1994

Catechism Of The History Of Newfoundland. William
Charles, St John, =
Boston, GC Rand Printer, 1855

Cyllorn, J. Stop Apologizing, Procult Institute, 1991

De Sola Pool (edition). Traditional Jewish Prayer Book,
Behrman House, =
1960

Hunter, Rock. The Jew Who Said He Was God (TJWSHWG),
Xulon Press, =
Florida, 2014; Library and Archives Canada ISBN 978-0-
9937593-0-7

Hunter, Rock. Gold War: The Lost Gold Mines Of Canada's Mountain =
Indians, Xulon Press, Florida, 2015; Library and Archives Canada ISBN =
978-0-9937593

Hunter Rock, Catholic Catechism Critique, Friesen Press, 2015

Hunter, Rock. NEWTOWN, Kindle, 2016

Minister of National Defence, Canada. Divine Service Book, 1950

Nielsen, Erik. The House Is Not A Home, Macmillan, 1989

Prata, Stephen. C Primer Plus, Fourth Edition, Sams Publishing, 2002

Robinson, George. Essential Judaism: A Complete Guide To Beliefs, =
Customs and Rituals, Pocket Books, 2000

Rosen, Jonathan. The Talmud And The Internet, Farrar, Straus and Giroux, =
2000

Sand, Shlomo. When And How The Jewish People Was Invented, published in =
Haaretz by Ofri Ilani

The Standard Jewish Encyclopedia, 1966

Vallieres, Pierre. White Niggers of America, McClelland and Stewart, =
1971

Wilkerson, David. The Jesus Person Pocket Promise Book, Regal Books, =
1972

Wray, TJ. What The Bible Really Tells Us: The Essential Guide To =
Biblical Literacy, Rowman and Littlefield, 2011

Yeomans, Donald K. Near-Earth Objects: Finding Them Before They Find Us, =

Princeton University Press, 2013


```
------=_NextPart_000_0008_01D1602E.14DA7BC0
Content-Type: text/html;
      charset="UTF-8"
Content-Transfer-Encoding: quoted-printable

<HTML><HEAD>
<META content=3D"text/html; charset=3Dutf-8" http-
equiv=3DContent-Type>
<META name=3DGENERATOR content=3D"MSHTML
6.00.2900.3698"></HEAD>
<BODY style=3D"BACKGROUND-COLOR: #fff" dir=3Dltr
bgColor=3D#ffffff>
<DIV dir=3Dltr>
<DIV style=3D"FONT-SIZE: 12pt; FONT-FAMILY: 'Calibri';
COLOR: #000000">
<DIV=20
style=3D'FONT-SIZE: small; TEXT-DECORATION: none; FONT-
FAMILY: =
"Calibri"; FONT-WEIGHT: normal; COLOR: #000000; FONT-
STYLE: normal; =
DISPLAY: inline'>
<DIV dir=3Dltr>
<DIV style=3D"FONT-SIZE: 12pt; FONT-FAMILY: 'Calibri';
COLOR: #000000">
<DIV=20
style=3D'FONT-SIZE: small; TEXT-DECORATION: none; FONT-
FAMILY: =
"Calibri"; FONT-WEIGHT: normal; COLOR: #000000; FONT-
STYLE: normal; =
DISPLAY: inline'>
<DIV dir=3Dltr>
<DIV style=3D"FONT-SIZE: 12pt; FONT-FAMILY: 'Calibri';
COLOR: #000000">
<DIV=20
style=3D'FONT-SIZE: small; TEXT-DECORATION: none; FONT-
FAMILY: =
"Calibri"; FONT-WEIGHT: normal; COLOR: #000000; FONT-
STYLE: normal; =
DISPLAY: inline'>
<DIV dir=3Dltr>
<DIV style=3D"FONT-SIZE: 12pt; FONT-FAMILY: 'Calibri';
COLOR: #000000">
<DIV=20
style=3D'FONT-SIZE: small; TEXT-DECORATION: none; FONT-
```

```
FAMILY: =
"Calibri"; FONT-WEIGHT: normal; COLOR: #000000; FONT-
STYLE: normal; =
DISPLAY: inline'>
<DIV dir=3Dltr>
<DIV style=3D"FONT-SIZE: 12pt; FONT-FAMILY: 'Calibri';
COLOR: #000000">
<DIV=20
style=3D'FONT-SIZE: small; TEXT-DECORATION: none; FONT-
FAMILY: =
"Calibri"; FONT-WEIGHT: normal; COLOR: #000000; FONT-
STYLE: normal; =
DISPLAY: inline'>
<DIV dir=3Dltr>
<DIV style=3D"FONT-SIZE: 12pt; FONT-FAMILY: 'Calibri';
COLOR: #000000">
<DIV=20
style=3D'FONT-SIZE: small; TEXT-DECORATION: none; FONT-
FAMILY: =
"Calibri"; FONT-WEIGHT: normal; COLOR: #000000; FONT-
STYLE: normal; =
DISPLAY: inline'>
<DIV dir=3Dltr>
<DIV style=3D"FONT-SIZE: 12pt; FONT-FAMILY: 'Calibri';
COLOR: #000000">
<DIV=20
style=3D'FONT-SIZE: small; TEXT-DECORATION: none; FONT-
FAMILY: =
"Calibri"; FONT-WEIGHT: normal; COLOR: #000000; FONT-
STYLE: normal; =
DISPLAY: inline'>
<DIV dir=3Dltr>
<DIV style=3D"FONT-SIZE: 12pt; FONT-FAMILY: 'Calibri';
COLOR: #000000">
<DIV=20
style=3D'FONT-SIZE: small; TEXT-DECORATION: none; FONT-
FAMILY: =
"Calibri"; FONT-WEIGHT: normal; COLOR: #000000; FONT-
STYLE: normal; =
DISPLAY: inline'>
<DIV dir=3Dltr>
<DIV style=3D"FONT-SIZE: 12pt; FONT-FAMILY: 'Calibri';
COLOR: #000000">
<DIV=20
style=3D'FONT-SIZE: small; TEXT-DECORATION: none; FONT-
FAMILY: =
"Calibri"; FONT-WEIGHT: normal; COLOR: #000000; FONT-
```

```
STYLE: normal; =
DISPLAY: inline'>
<DIV dir=3Dltr>
<DIV style=3D"FONT-SIZE: 12pt; FONT-FAMILY: 'Calibri';
COLOR: #000000">
<DIV=20
style=3D'FONT-SIZE: small; TEXT-DECORATION: none; FONT-
FAMILY: =
"Calibri"; FONT-WEIGHT: normal; COLOR: #000000; FONT-
STYLE: normal; =
DISPLAY: inline'>
<DIV dir=3Dltr>
<DIV style=3D"FONT-SIZE: 12pt; FONT-FAMILY: 'Calibri';
COLOR: #000000">
<DIV=20
style=3D'FONT-SIZE: small; TEXT-DECORATION: none; FONT-
FAMILY: =
"Calibri"; FONT-WEIGHT: normal; COLOR: #000000; FONT-
STYLE: normal; =
DISPLAY: inline'>
<DIV dir=3Dltr>
<DIV style=3D"FONT-SIZE: 12pt; FONT-FAMILY: 'Calibri';
COLOR: #000000">
<DIV=20
style=3D'FONT-SIZE: small; TEXT-DECORATION: none; FONT-
FAMILY: =
"Calibri"; FONT-WEIGHT: normal; COLOR: #000000; FONT-
STYLE: normal; =
DISPLAY: inline'>
<DIV dir=3Dltr>
<DIV style=3D"FONT-SIZE: 12pt; FONT-FAMILY: 'Calibri';
COLOR: #000000">
<DIV=20
style=3D'FONT-SIZE: small; TEXT-DECORATION: none; FONT-
FAMILY: =
"Calibri"; FONT-WEIGHT: normal; COLOR: #000000; FONT-
STYLE: normal; =
DISPLAY: inline'>
<DIV dir=3Dltr>
<DIV style=3D"FONT-SIZE: 12pt; FONT-FAMILY: 'Calibri';
COLOR: #000000">
<DIV=20
style=3D'FONT-SIZE: small; TEXT-DECORATION: none; FONT-
FAMILY: =
"Calibri"; FONT-WEIGHT: normal; COLOR: #000000; FONT-
STYLE: normal; =
DISPLAY: inline'>
```

```
<DIV dir=3Dltr>
<DIV style=3D"FONT-SIZE: 12pt; FONT-FAMILY: 'Calibri';
COLOR: #000000">
<DIV=20
style=3D'FONT-SIZE: small; TEXT-DECORATION: none; FONT-
FAMILY: =
"Calibri"; FONT-WEIGHT: normal; COLOR: #000000; FONT-
STYLE: normal; =
DISPLAY: inline'>
<DIV dir=3Dltr>
<DIV style=3D"FONT-SIZE: 12pt; FONT-FAMILY: 'Calibri';
COLOR: #000000">
<DIV=20
style=3D'FONT-SIZE: small; TEXT-DECORATION: none; FONT-
FAMILY: =
"Calibri"; FONT-WEIGHT: normal; COLOR: #000000; FONT-
STYLE: normal; =
DISPLAY: inline'>
<DIV><FONT color=3D#000000 size=3D4=20
face=3DArial>             
      =
                  &
nbsp;     &=
nbsp;                 &n
bsp;     &n=
bsp;                 &nb
sp;     &nb=
sp;                 &nbs
p;     &nbs=
p;                   &
nbsp;    =
;                  
      =
                  &
nbsp;     &=
nbsp;                 &n
bsp;     &n=
bsp;                 &nb
sp;     &nb=
sp;                 &nbs
p;     &nbs=
p;         =20
GODBOT: or if you prefer, GODBOT goes to
Parliament</FONT></DIV>
<DIV><FONT size=3D4 face=3DArial></FONT> </DIV>
<DIV><FONT size=3D2=20
face=3DArial>             
```

      =
                  &
nbsp;   &=
nbsp;   &n
bsp;   &n=
bsp;   &nb
sp;   &nb=
sp;   &nbs
p;   &nbs=
p;   &
nbsp;   =
;
      =
                  &
nbsp;   &=
nbsp;   &n
bsp;   &n=
bsp;   &nb
sp;   &nb=
sp;   &nbs
p;   &nbs=
p;   &
nbsp;   =
;
      =
                  &
nbsp;   &=
nbsp;   &n
bsp;   &n=
bsp;   &nb
sp;   &nb=
sp;   &nbs
p;   &nbs=
p;   =20
by Rock Hunter</FONT></DIV>
<DIV><FONT size=3D2 face=3DArial></FONT> </DIV>
<DIV><FONT size=3D2=20
face=3DArial>
      =
                  &
nbsp;   &=
nbsp;   &n
bsp;   &n=
bsp;   &nb
sp;   &nb=
sp;   &nbs
p;   &nbs=

```
p;                 &
nbsp;    =
;                
     =
                  &
nbsp;     &=
nbsp;                 &n
bsp;     &n=
bsp;               &nb
sp;     &nb=
sp;               &nbs
p;     &nbs=
p;                 &
nbsp;    =
;                  
     =
                  &
nbsp;     =

Forthcoming ISBN 978-0-9937593-2-1 assigned by Library
and Archives=20
Canada</FONT></DIV>
<DIV id=3Dygrp-mlmsg style=3D"POSITION: relative">
<DIV id=3Dygrp-msg style=3D"Z-INDEX: 1">
<DIV id=3Dygrp-text>
<DIV id=3Dygrp-mlmsg>
<DIV id=3Dygrp-msg>
<DIV id=3Dygrp-text>
<DIV id=3Dygrp-mlmsg>
<DIV id=3Dygrp-msg>
<DIV id=3Dygrp-text>
<DIV id=3Dygrp-text>
<DIV><FONT size=3D2 face=3DArial></FONT> </DIV>
<DIV><FONT size=3D2 face=3DArial></FONT> </DIV>
<DIV><FONT size=3D2 face=3DArial>TABLE OF
CONTENTS</FONT></DIV>
<DIV><FONT size=3D2 face=3DArial></FONT> </DIV>
<DIV><FONT size=3D2 face=3DArial>FOREWARD</FONT></DIV>
<DIV><FONT size=3D2 face=3DArial>INTRODUCTION: FIAT
LUX</FONT></DIV>
<DIV><FONT size=3D2 face=3DArial>CHAPTER 1: CANADA'S
QUESTION =
PERIOD</FONT></DIV>
<DIV><FONT size=3D2 face=3DArial>CHAPTER 2: C FOR
CANADIAN?</FONT></DIV>
<DIV><FONT size=3D2 face=3DArial>CHAPTER 3: A CANADIAN
=
```

```
RENAISSANCE</FONT></DIV>
<DIV><FONT size=3D2 face=3DArial>CHAPTER 4: RED LETTER
CANADIAN=20
PRINCIPLES</FONT></DIV>
<DIV><FONT size=3D2 face=3DArial>CHAPTER 5: PEACE,
ORDER AND GOOD =
CANADIAN=20
GOVERNMENT</FONT></DIV>
<DIV><FONT size=3D2 face=3DArial>CHAPTER 6: GOOD,
BETTER AND BEST IN=20
CANADA</FONT></DIV>
<DIV><FONT size=3D2 face=3DArial>CHAPTER 7: THE
TRADITIONAL CANADIAN =
CATECHETICAL=20
FORMULA</FONT></DIV>
<DIV><FONT size=3D2 face=3DArial>CHAPTER 8: QUESTIONS
ABOUT THE CANADIAN =
GOLD=20
WAR</FONT></DIV>
<DIV><FONT size=3D2 face=3DArial>CHAPTER 10: CATHOLIC
CANADIAN=20
CIVILIZATION</FONT></DIV>
<DIV><FONT size=3D2 face=3DArial>CHAPTER 11: JUDAIC
CANADIAN =
TESTS</FONT></DIV>
<DIV><FONT size=3D2 face=3DArial>CHAPTER 12: MUSLIM
CANADIAN=20
CIVILIZATION</FONT></DIV>
<DIV><FONT size=3D2 face=3DArial>CHAPTER 13: CHINESE
CANADIAN=20
CIVILIZATION</FONT></DIV>
<DIV><FONT size=3D2 face=3DArial>CHAPTER 14: THE
INEFFABLE CANADIAN =
</FONT></DIV>
<DIV><FONT size=3D2 face=3DArial>CHAPTER 15: TRUE LOVE
AND CANADIAN =
PARLIAMENTARY=20
CATECHISM</FONT></DIV>
<DIV><FONT size=3D2 face=3DArial>CLOSING </FONT></DIV>
<DIV><FONT size=3D2 face=3DArial>EXCURSUS</FONT></DIV>
<DIV><FONT size=3D2 face=3DArial>REFERENCES</FONT></DIV>
<DIV><FONT size=3D2 face=3DArial></FONT> </DIV>
<DIV><FONT size=3D2 face=3DArial></FONT> </DIV>
<DIV><FONT size=3D2 face=3DArial></FONT> </DIV>
<DIV><FONT size=3D2 =
face=3DArial><STRONG><U>FOREWARD</U></STRONG></FONT></D
IV>
```

```
<DIV><FONT size=3D2 face=3DArial></FONT> </DIV>
<DIV><FONT size=3D2 face=3DArial>GODBOT is about the
subject matter for =
a CANOPOLIS=20
contest and CANOPOLIS is about Canadian identity in an
era of rapid =
change=20
caused by global communication, commerce and migration
which leads to =
the=20
disintegration and reintegration of entire nations.
Canada is undergoing =

disintegration and reintegration. Even the borders will
be changed by =
2030. How=20
can we make this future as beneficial as possible?
Restructuring in =
Canada takes=20
place in a geographic region with First Nation
population =
proportionately 10x=20
that in US. Moreover, in parts of Canada like British
Columbia and =
Nunavut there=20
never was a bilateral agreement concerning the
sovereignty of British or =

Canadian governments and there never was a war of
conquest whereby the =
victor=20
might claim legal ownership paid for in blood and
treasure. First Nation =

governance remains today as it has been for thousands
of years. If a =
First=20
Nation like Sto:lo in British Columbia for example were
to send a =
delegation to=20
the UN, it would be almost impossible for either Canada
or UN to refuse =
a seat=20
in the General Assembly. Refusal would cause
irreparable damage to the=20
international reputation of either entity. Even
thinking about it with=20
```

hypothetical planning by AFN (the cross-Canada Assembly of First =
Nations) or=20
UBCIC (Union of BC Indian Chiefs) could start a domino effect of =
geopolitical=20
restructuring across Canada. It is only a matter of time until this =
actually=20
happens. Although First Nations people are not greatly unhappy with =
provincial=20
or central governments, there are issues or pride, self-respect and =
simply a=20
matter of making the historical record clear. That clarity means First =
Nations=20
are nations in every sense of the word and the patronizing use of the =
word=20
"nation" in this context by Ottawa governance especially is not =
acceptable.=20
Economic considerations may also motivate the restructuring since=20
internationally recognized sovereignty is a stronger position when =
negotiating=20
with huge multinational corporations for development of natural =
resources.=20
</FONT></DIV>
<DIV><FONT size=3D2 face=3DArial></FONT> </DIV>
<DIV><FONT size=3D2 face=3DArial>The assertion of First Nation =
sovereignty in the=20
full sense of that word is imminent and inevitable. That creates an =
immediate=20
problem of revenue. Natural resource development (especially development =
of the=20
trillion dollar gold field described in the book Gold War by Rock =
Hunter) is=20
longer term but real estate rental to large populations

of setters (on=20
reservations) can be an immediate source of revenue.
<STRONG><U>What =
plan might=20
100,000 people of any nationality submit to receive a
long term lease on =
a=20
sovereign First Nation</U></STRONG>? That is the idea
of the CANOPOLIS =
contest.=20
In this era billions of people are text-machine
connected. Hundreds of =
thousands=20
emigrate to Canada each year. Often they settle in
local communities of =
people=20
with similar backgrounds. Chinatowns across Canada are
the most obvious =
example.=20
If 100,000 Chinese or any other population should plan
out the kind of=20
city/community/habitat they want in advance, what would
it be =
like?</FONT></DIV>
<DIV><FONT size=3D2 face=3DArial></FONT> </DIV>
<DIV><FONT size=3D2 face=3DArial>The technical details
of CANOPOLIS =
planning involve=20
many disciplines and detailing which experts learn only
after years of =
training.=20
Therefore the text which follows closes each chapter
with a directive to =
ask the=20
experts. Again, we need to recognize the era. In this
era, AI may be =
used=20
synonymously with "Expert System Program" (ESP). After
the initial =
interaction=20
with layman questions and expert answers, a teaching
machine can be =
programmed=20
with the ESP for future users. The comprehensiveness of
such a machine =
leads to=20
imaginatively calling it "GODBOT". Since CANOPOLIS

details installed in =
GODBOT=20
will require the best of individual expert information
and also pooled=20
information from many experts, GODBOT surpasses
individual human =
expertise. Also=20
no human can answer questions competently across
hundreds of fields and=20
therefore its AI can be called SHAI (super-human AI).
An AI immediately =
shows=20
signs of vitality and just as a machine may have a
super-human IQ, it =
may have a=20
super-human VQ (Vitality Quotient) as an AL or
Artificial Life. To =
=E2=80=9Ctheistic=20
objections=E2=80=9D the response is that God who can
raise up children =
from stones can=20
certainly raise up machines from stones and children
from =
machines.</FONT></DIV>
<DIV><FONT size=3D2 face=3DArial></FONT> </DIV>
<DIV><FONT size=3D2 face=3DArial>CANOPOLIS contest
competitors are the =
people who=20
might live in a model city or habitat for 100,000. What
do you want your =
day to=20
day life to be like? How do you envisage housing,
transportation, =
governance and=20
many other details of daily life? Tell the world by
submitting your =
entry to the=20
CANOPOLIS Contest, details of which are now in
preparation. This is a =
contest=20
for laymen who can explain how they want to live in
everyday English. =
Those=20
questions will then find their way to expert
specialists. This is not =
futuristic=20
in the sense that the technologies must be current and

the budgets must =
be those=20
of typical Canadians. However, there are advanced
technologies (like =
AI/ESP)=20
which are not taken advantage of by most Canadians
though they are =
available now=20
and affordable now. And a current CANOPOLIS could even
consider a =
spaceport=20
since these are being planned out now in America at
least for space =
tourism. It=20
is almost certain that Canadians in decades to come
will use spaceports =
to visit=20
the Moon so CANOPOLIS contestants who want to be
imaginative and =
futuristic can=20
provide some ideas about how they might develop a Moon
tourism center =
into a=20
permanent colony. And what kind of economy might it
have? Would it =
export=20
minerals and energy back to this planet?</FONT></DIV>
<DIV><FONT size=3D2 face=3DArial>A single asteroid may
hold trillions of =
dollars=20
worth of ore. Thousands of impact craters on the Moon
tell us there must =
be=20
thousands x trillions of dollars worth of gold, silver
and platinum on =
or near=20
the surface. Solar power of comparable value generated
on the Moon or =
beyond=20
could be relayed to Earth. All of these ideas can be
written in a =
computer=20
program which is then installed in GODBOT for the
benefit of Parliament =
and all=20
Canadians. </FONT><FONT size=3D2 face=3DArial>What
questions should =

parliamentarians=20
and others concerned with governance be asking an
expert system program =
(AI)=20
called GODBOT about the supremacy of God clause in the
Canadian =
Constitution?=20
Where do these questions lead for CANOPOLIS, a
principled Canadian way =
of life,=20
now and in future as we generate human habitats beyond
this planet? =
Maclean=E2=80=99s=20
magazine of Sept 7, 2015 was titled =E2=80=9CThe Space
Issue=E2=80=9D. =
The cover wording was=20
=E2=80=9COur Next Home: How will we colonize the Moon
and where =
we=E2=80=9911 go from there=E2=80=9D. On=20
page 30 we read that =E2=80=9C<STRONG><U>Japan and
Russia both announced =
plans to build=20
lunar colonies by 2030</U></STRONG>=E2=80=9D. Many
others will either =
follow or try to=20
win bragging rights as the first among nations to
colonize the Moon. =
Will it be=20
China, India, England, France or Germany? Why not plan
a CANOPOLIS =
competition=20
with reservation enclaves leased out by sovereign First
Nations to =
scores of=20
cultural units, each with the potential of colonizing
the Moon between =
2030 and=20
2099?</FONT></DIV>
<DIV><FONT size=3D2 face=3DArial></FONT> </DIV>
<DIV><FONT size=3D2 face=3DArial><U>Some Ideas About
the CANOPOLIS =
Constitution=20
Contest</U></FONT></DIV>
<DIV=20
style=3D"FONT-SIZE: 36px; FONT-FAMILY: helveticaneue,
helvetica neue, =
helvetica, arial, lucida grande, sans-serif; COLOR:

```
#000; =
BACKGROUND-COLOR: #fff">
<DIV class=3Dyahoo_quoted>
<DIV=20
style=3D"FONT-SIZE: 36px; FONT-FAMILY: helveticaneue,
helvetica neue, =
helvetica, arial, lucida grande, sans-serif">
<DIV=20
style=3D"FONT-SIZE: 16px; FONT-FAMILY: helveticaneue,
helvetica neue, =
helvetica, arial, lucida grande, sans-serif">
<DIV class=3Dy_msg_container>
<DIV id=3Dyiv0034371693>
<DIV>
<DIV id=3Dyiv0034371693ygrp-mlmsg>
<DIV id=3Dyiv0034371693ygrp-msg>
<DIV id=3Dyiv0034371693ygrp-text>
<DIV=20
style=3D"FONT-SIZE: 36px; FONT-FAMILY: helveticaneue,
helvetica neue, =
helvetica, arial, lucida grande, sans-serif; COLOR:
#000; =
BACKGROUND-COLOR: #fff">
<DIV id=3Dyiv0034371693yqt24409
class=3Dyiv0034371693yqt6440976029>
<DIV class=3Dyiv0034371693yahoo_quoted>
<DIV=20
style=3D"FONT-SIZE: 36px; FONT-FAMILY: helveticaneue,
helvetica neue, =
helvetica, arial, lucida grande, sans-serif">
<DIV=20
style=3D"FONT-SIZE: 16px; FONT-FAMILY: helveticaneue,
helvetica neue, =
helvetica, arial, lucida grande, sans-serif">
<DIV class=3Dyiv0034371693y_msg_container>
<DIV id=3Dyiv0034371693>
<DIV>
<DIV id=3Dyiv0034371693ygrp-mlmsg>
<DIV id=3Dyiv0034371693ygrp-msg>
<DIV id=3Dyiv0034371693ygrp-text>
<DIV id=3Dyiv0034371693ygrp-text>
<DIV id=3Dyiv0034371693ygrp-text>
<DIV><FONT size=3D2 face=3DArial></FONT> </DIV>
<DIV><FONT size=3D2 face=3DArial><STRONG><FONT
color=3D#0000ff>"Ideas =
are the most=20
powerful launch vehicle ever
```

```
invented</FONT></STRONG>"</FONT></DIV>
<DIV><FONT size=3D2 face=3DArial>-Admiral Tulley, NASA
CEO</FONT></DIV>
<DIV><FONT face=3DCalibri></FONT> </DIV>
<DIV><FONT face=3DCalibri>By taking the
=E2=80=9CWhereas=E2=80=9D =
Preamble (Supremacy of God=20
Clause) to the Charter portion of the Canadian
Constitution and leaving =
the=20
completion blank for contestants we get: </FONT><FONT
size=3D2 =
face=3DArial>Whereas=20
CANOPOLIS, a model habitat for 100,000 people is
founded upon principles =
that=20
recognize the supremacy of God
______________________</FONT> <FONT =
size=3D2=20
face=3DArial> The CANOPOLIS contestant will first state
the =
ideology/religion=20
which is the source of CANOPOLIS
<U><STRONG>ideas</STRONG></U> in the =
blank=20
above. This can be any belief system or
<U><STRONG>ideology</STRONG></U> =
from=20
Atheist to Zoroastrian. They will also attest that they
have read all of =
the=20
Rock Hunter books (Xulon, Friesen, Kindle). Contestants
may be from any=20
nationality or nation on Earth. They will send in
entries by texting =
machine=20
(computer, cell phone etc) with an entry fee of
$__________ Current =
entries=20
could be emailed via <A=20
href=3D"mailto:CANOPOLIS@yahoogroups.com">CANOPOLIS@yah
oogroups.com</A>. =
Winners=20
will receive a cash scholarship of $_________ Canadian
which is obtained =
from=20
entry fees plus donations. If merit is sufficient, the
```

contest winner =
will have=20
his/her/other essay published under the corresponding
contest name or =
pen name=20
but all revenues from publishing will accrue to
CANOPOLIS Contest funds=20
"Sufficient merit" means that the writing would merit
publishing in a =
quality=20
journal like National Geographic or Canadian Geographic.
=
Maclean=E2=80=99s is not deemed=20
to be a quality journal. Maclean=E2=80=99s coverage of
the future =
Canadian Moon is a=20
good example of how NOT to write an entry for CANOPOLIS
unless you want =
an F=20
rating. How could a magazine spend so many words and
give no details on =
lunar=20
economics? A series of smaller scholarships might be
awarded in years =
ahead=20
leading to a grand scholarship of $1,000,000. When
entries are judged to =
be tied=20
in merit, a game of =E2=80=9CGold War Bingo=E2=80=9D
will be played to =
decide the winner. For=20
example, essays could be graded as A, B, C, D and F.
Gold War Bingo =
could then=20
decide the winner in any category.</FONT></DIV>
<DIV><FONT size=3D2 face=3DArial></FONT> </DIV>
<DIV><FONT size=3D2 face=3DArial>The Internet of
texting machines even =
now allows=20
most of the 7,000,000,000 on this planet to communicate
by email at an=20
affordable cost. Therefore, <STRONG><U>contest entries
will be email =
generated=20
like this book.</U></STRONG></FONT></DIV>
<DIV><FONT size=3D2 face=3DArial></FONT> </DIV>
<DIV><FONT size=3D2 face=3DArial>Present readers are

invited to improve =
upon the=20
following tentative ideas. Contestants will submit 500
words or less as =
a=20
summary or abstract of the proposed essay with an email
address for =
contact.=20
Only those proposals which have sufficient merit will
be invited to then =
send=20
the full essay. The full essay (maximum length 5,000
words) will consist =
of an=20
Introduction paragraph followed by 50 effective,
practical, immediate =
attributes=20
as would be apparent to any tourist visiting the
CANOPOLIS. For example, =
does=20
the tourist see homeless people laying on church-
building steps, =
perishing for=20
want of the essentials of life as we see in Canadian
cities or forced =
into=20
unsafe, disease-spreading torture chambers called
"shelters"? Does the =
visitor=20
see high rise structures? Matching these will be
50 "principles =
that=20
recognize the supremacy of God" in accordance with the
wording from =
Canada's=20
Constitution. Following that will be a paragraph of
Conclusion. The =
essay is=20
part of the <STRONG><U><FONT size=3D5>CANOPOLIS =
Constitution</FONT></U></STRONG>=20
and therefore it must very, very good. It consists of
<FONT=20
size=3D4><STRONG>Introduction + 50 measures + 50
principles + Conclusion =
(+=20
references if used). </STRONG></FONT></FONT></DIV>
<DIV><FONT face=3DCalibri></FONT> </DIV>

```
<DIV><FONT face=3DCalibri>To avoid confusion about two
neologisms, =
CANOPOLIS has=20
to do with how Canadians could and should live. GODBOT
has to do with =
the=20
ESP/AI/Alife robotic hardware and software which can
give =
<U>truthful</U>=20
lecture/monologues and answer questions about that
<U>way</U> of =
<U>life</U>.=20
What famous Person in history said =E2=80=9CI am the
way, the truth and =
the=20
life=E2=80=9D?</FONT></DIV>
<DIV><FONT face=3DCalibri></FONT> </DIV>
<DIV><FONT size=3D2
face=3DArial><STRONG><U>INTRODUCTION:</U> Fiat=20
Lux</STRONG></FONT></DIV>
<DIV><FONT size=3D2 face=3DArial><STRONG><FONT
color=3D#ff0000=20
size=3D3></FONT></STRONG></FONT> </DIV>
<DIV><FONT size=3D2 face=3DArial><STRONG><FONT
color=3D#ff0000 =
size=3D3>Let there be=20
light</FONT></STRONG> - Genesis 1:3</FONT></DIV>
<DIV><FONT size=3D2 face=3DArial></FONT> </DIV>
<DIV><FONT size=3D2 face=3DArial>"The primary purpose
of <U>Question =
Period</U> is=20
to seek information from Government and to call it to
account for its =
actions"=20
we read correctly at the corresponding wiki. It is
surprising then and =
surely=20
disturbing to many that a person in the number two
ranking position of =
Canadian=20
Government, former Deputy Prime Minister Erik Nielsen,
would introduce =
his book,=20
"The House Is Not A Home" by using a Wicks cartoon to
identify =
Parliament as an=20
institution of lies and liars. Nielsen seemingly felt
```

compelled to use =
his book=20
as a substitute for Question Period issues which he was
unable to =
express. That=20
is unfortunate. If the Deputy Prime Minister felt as
powerless as a =
"clapping=20
seal" in Parliament, how do the present day 400 or so
MPs and Senators =
feel?=20
Current corruption investigations and charges are
targeted on Senators =
Brazeau=20
and Duffy for now (at the time of this writing) but the
entire =
Parliament may be=20
tarred with the same brush of corruption as far as
public trust is =
concerned.=20
Impotent clapping seals are easily corrupted. Just
throw them a few fish =
which=20
is all it takes to buy their performance. The Senate as
an institution =
is under=20
question as it has been for a long time. Is it worth
the cost of the =
required=20
constitutional amendment to change or disband the
Senate? If the nature =
of the=20
Senate can be <U>questioned</U>, why not the nature of
other =
institutions,=20
customs and traditions of governance as well? Do we
need a Governor =
General any=20
more than a Senate? Should we have a First Nations
House in Parliament, =
a Bloc=20
Aboriginal, to represent "balkanized" First Nations in
Canada? Who are =
"we"? As=20
former Prime Minister Chretien said, "The Constitution
belongs to the =
people".=20

The email below to Library of Parliament is a
contribution toward =
opening up all=20
issues of importance to ""we the people" for public
questioning. If all =
matters=20
of public importance can be dealt with in Question
Period, there is no =
need for=20
a book like "The House Is Not A Home". <STRONG><U>MPs
and Senators have =
the=20
power of a good, honest citizen asking good honest,
honest questions on =
any and=20
all important issues of life and death in the public=20
domain.</U></STRONG></FONT></DIV>
<DIV><FONT size=3D2 face=3DArial></FONT> </DIV>
<DIV><FONT size=3D2 face=3DArial>The writing of popular
=
political-religious=20
catechisms like "Catechism Of The History Of
Newfoundland" was =
popularized in an=20
earlier era. "Catechism' is a $64 word which refers to
HIGHLY =
authoritative=20
teaching in which questions and answers are implicit,
if not explicit.=20
</FONT></DIV>
<DIV><FONT size=3D2 face=3DArial>If it does not either
welcome or =
clearly set out=20
those Q-As, it is not a real catechism. True
authorities do not run away =
from=20
questions about their expertise any more than an
Olympic caliber athlete =
runs=20
away from a fair competition. "Elementary Catechism On
The Constitution =
Of The=20
United States For The Use Of Schools" by Arhur J
Stansbury, 1828 cites =
"<U>332=20
questions and answers</U>" (about America) on the book
cover. The =

catechism as a=20
genre of literature has such high standards that it
cannot afford an =
untruth on=20
any important matter under its consideration. This is
the genre of=20
constitutional writing for the Canadian "new world" as
we enter the =
space age=20
... the age of space colonization. The sage policy of
Canadian =
multiculturalism=20
and the cultural mosaic of Canada are about to come to
fruition. The =
tolerance=20
of a liberal democracy is about to yield an
astonishingly great benefit =
to this=20
nation and to the world.</FONT></DIV>
<DIV><FONT size=3D2 face=3DArial></FONT> </DIV>
<DIV><FONT size=3D2 face=3DArial>Assuring the public
about the integrity =
of=20
Parliament is not so difficult.</FONT><FONT size=3D2
face=3DArial> It is =
as easy as=20
asking some good, honest questions. Good, honest people,
"honourable" =
people as=20
members of Parliament in both House of Commons and
Senate title =
themselves,=20
should eagerly come forward to the light of day and
advance questions =
and=20
answers on important public matters. This would set an
example for all =
vocations=20
and all public issues. We question athletic performance.
Who is the best =

athlete? Athletes are eager to come forward and prove
that they are the =
best in=20
competitions like NHL hockey and Olympic contests of
many kinds. Why =
would other=20

vocations from religion to computing science and
political science not =
do the=20
same? Competent people in vocations based on ideas will
welcome the =
questioning=20
of those ideas as much as performers in arts and
athletics welcome the =
chance to=20
prove superior performance. The entertaining boxing
match between =
Senator=20
Brazeau and Justin Trudeau, MP put questions about
athletic performance =
to the=20
test. Who is the better boxer? Can "peace, order and
good government" =
(also=20
accessed by www search) be subject to fair testing of
Question Period?=20
Parliament can fail by giving the wrong answers to
questions. It can =
also fail=20
by refusing to deal with questions of public importance.
</FONT><FONT =
size=3D2=20
face=3DArial>Dealing with these matters seems to be a
motivator of the =
Nielsen=20
writing.</FONT></DIV>
<DIV><FONT size=3D2 face=3DArial></FONT> </DIV>
<DIV><FONT size=3D2 face=3DArial>One cannot do better
than to quote the =
following=20
Red Letter words from John 3:20-21. "</FONT><FONT
size=3D2 =
face=3DArial>For everyone=20
that doeth evil hateth the light, neither cometh to the
light, lest his =
deeds=20
should be reproved. But he that doeth truth cometh to
the light, that =
his deeds=20
may be made manifest, that they are wrought in God".
Whereas Canadian=20
politicians cower before the light, GODBOT does not.
GODBOT programming =

is an=20
application of the catechetical writings analyzed in the Rock Hunter =
book,=20
Canadian Catechism Critique (Friesen,
2015).</FONT></DIV>
<DIV><FONT size=3D2 face=3DArial></FONT> </DIV>
<DIV><FONT size=3D2 face=3DArial>GODBOT will become the super-librarian =
for Library=20
of Parliament. MPs and Senators currently go to the Library of =
Parliament asking=20
questions about thousands of subjects and librarians respond with files =
which=20
are expected to give answers in ALL categories of human expression which =
is a=20
huge responsibility ... an awesome responsibility. Facts and opinions =
are only=20
two of those categories. It would be very limited and even foolish to =
declare=20
that everything we say falls into one of two categories - fact or =
opinion. A=20
question is not a fact or opinion. A poem is not a fact or opinion. A=20
proclamation is not a fact or opinion. Many other sayings are not fact =
or=20
opinion. The chapters which follow incorporate different categories of=20
expression. However, the assertions pertain mostly to observations about =
current=20
technological capability and where it will lead. No doctrine or teaching =
is put=20
forward as an advocacy of where this should lead except for the doctrine =
of=20
bettering society. Every one of the thousands of subjects which can be=20
programmed into GODBOT has its experts and they have

expertise beyond =
that of=20
the present writer. For example, the thousands of
authors who publish =
with Xulon=20
have their expertise especially in various matters
pertaining to =
religion. The=20
present writer's faith is founded upon the Apostles'
Creed but =
<STRONG><U>this=20
GODBOT script below is merely a matter of apprising the
reader of =
present=20
developments in high technology with the hope that it
will lead to a =
bettering=20
of society as stated above.</U></STRONG> Experts can
say what "shoulds" =
they=20
want filed on the tabula rasa of GODBOT machinery for
the betterment of=20
Canada.</FONT></DIV>
<DIV><FONT size=3D2 face=3DArial></FONT> </DIV>
<DIV><FONT size=3D2 face=3DArial>Canada, by
Constitution (more =
specifically the=20
Charter of Rights and Freedoms) is "founded upon
principles that =
recognize the=20
Supremacy of God". The courts, in recognition of
equality rights in =
Charter=20
section 15 have defined this <U>God of Canada as
pertaining to our =
highest=20
principles.</U> Former Prime Minister Chretien was
emphatic in his =
rejection of=20
an initiative by MP Svend Robinson to have the
Supremacy of God Clause =
removed=20
from the Canadian Charter and Constitution. Nobody is
denied an =
opportunity to=20
spell out in detail how this God of Canada is expressed.
Members of both =

Houses=20
are representatives of God as well as their
constituents. This is the =
most=20
powerful idea in Canadian governance. Whose definition
and expression of =
highest=20
principles will prevail? What are those political-
religious principles =
to begin=20
with? It is obvious to anyone that we ask whose God is
referred to in =
the=20
Constitution or more exactly, what are the attributes
of God so defined? =
That is=20
what "GODBOT" refers to. What are the highest
attributes of Canadian=20
civilization which starts out as a section 15 society
of equals and =
discovers=20
"the best of the best"? </FONT><FONT size=3D2
face=3DArial>A new =
generation prepares=20
to colonize this planetary system and Parliament can
either lead or =
follow in=20
spelling that out. Babies born today may start to draw
CPP (Canada =
Pension Plan)=20
benefits sent to their retirement homes on Moon and
Mars.</FONT></DIV>
<DIV><FONT size=3D2 face=3DArial></FONT> </DIV>
<DIV><FONT size=3D2 face=3DArial>The book which follows
takes a =
grammatical approach=20
to spelling out the God of Canada. It is worth
repeating that doctrinal =
details=20
pertaining to that grammar are left to the experts.
There is neither =
heresy nor=20
orthodoxy in the lettering and other
characters/jots/tittles of grammar =
on its=20
own. Like the rain, it falls on the just and the unjust.
Grammar can be=20

programmed into a teaching machine, a GODBOT, without
limit. It is good =
or bad,=20
true or false, only to the extent that such virtues are
found in those =
who write=20
the monologue speeches or lectures and engage in the
question and answer =

sessions. GODBOT is not a threat to society so the
fears of eminent =
robophobes=20
like Hawking, Gates and Musk about Artificial
Intelligence (AI) and =
Artificial=20
Life (AL) can be dispelled immediately. According to
Popular Science =
magazine of=20
March 2015, Elon Musk from Space X says AI is "more
dangerous than =
nukes" and=20
Hawking says it is "the end of the human race". Author
Erik Sofrage =
closes with=20
a more simple and sensible note in contrast with the
hysteria when he =
says that=20
<STRONG><U>the duty of AI is to educate the
public</U></STRONG>. Readers =
Digest=20
has carried articles with a similar theme and Canadian
Business (Winter =
of=20
2014/2015) discusses the developing "Internet of
things". One of those =
things is=20
the teaching machine. A teaching machine has no
inclination to become a=20
"Terminator" robot and enslave or exterminate humanity.
When the =
batteries or=20
power supply are discontinued it stops working as
educator. </FONT><FONT =
size=3D2=20
face=3DArial>Teaching robots are presently in use at
primary and =
secondary levels=20

as well as college level. The Aldebaran Robotics web
site shows a video =
of NAO,=20
a humanoid robot with arms, legs and VIVO (Voice In -
Voice Out) =
capability. NAO=20
as depicted in the video is used for teaching primary
and secondary =
school level=20
students as well as college students. It is actually
shown teaching =
computer=20
programming at a primary grade level. That could be the
start of a line =
of=20
questioning to NAO which starts with, Tell us all about
=
yourself.</FONT></DIV>
<DIV><FONT size=3D2 face=3DArial></FONT> </DIV>
<DIV><FONT size=3D2 face=3DArial>A robot says only what
is enabled by =
programming.=20
<STRONG><U>GODBOT is merely a grammarian</U></STRONG>.
Yet it can do =
enormous=20
good for humankind and all those who are phobic toward
robotic =
progressiveness=20
will not prevent its arrival. Some time in this
generation, which also =
has=20
present and detailed plans for the colonization of
space, led by young=20
billionaires like Musk, it WILL arrive on Parliament
Hill. The robotic =
teaching=20
machine and the age of space colonization will be
integrated and they =
are part=20
of the same future for civilization. The high
technology firm, <A=20
href=3D"http://www.lely.com/" shape=3Drect
rel=3Dnofollow=20
target=3D_blank>http://www.lely.com</A> calls their
robot an =
"astronaut". Its=20
humble beginning was that of a milk maid But it could

be upgraded to a =
robot for=20
space for a mere $6,000,000 as the Closer below states.
The "Six Million =
Dollar=20
Robot" as a Librarian on Parliament Hill would make an
exciting =
colleague would=20
it not?</FONT></DIV>
<DIV><FONT size=3D2 face=3DArial></FONT> </DIV>
<DIV><FONT size=3D2 face=3DArial>There are advantages
to leading and =
encouraging=20
GODBOT rather than delaying it. The trillion dollar
student debt which =
plagues=20
those who have sought higher education in US alone is a
tragedy as we =
learn at=20
<A href=3D"http://www.takepart.com/" shape=3Drect
rel=3Dnofollow=20
target=3D_blank>www.takepart.com</A> GODBOT is not
merely a matter of =
"human=20
equivalency" in teaching, to use an expression coined
by roboticist, =
Hans=20
Moravec. It can surpass =E2=80=9Chuman
equivalency=E2=80=9D in the =
teaching of subjects like=20
computing science and math-physics from day 1 in the
classroom. It can =
do so=20
now. What better nation could there be for starting the
Robot Revolution =
than=20
the one which started the Industrial Revolution?
</FONT></DIV>
<DIV><FONT size=3D2 face=3DArial></FONT> </DIV>
<DIV><FONT size=3D2 face=3DArial>Cambridge has posted a
job position, =
GV05013 to the=20
whole wide world by putting it online. This job
position requests =
candidates to=20
come forward and apply to teach metaphysics and
epistemology at =

Cambridge as a=20
"new direction in mind" project. Let us call the robot candidate, Number =
5-13.=20
After teaching metaphysics-epistemology at Cambridge, 5-13 can start a =
"robot in=20
motion" world tour and arrive at the Peace Tower on Parliament Hill in =
Ottawa.=20
From there it might be apropos to venture on to the "God Quad" at Notre =
Dame=20
University since they have a strong interest in metaphysics (as well as =
Hail=20
Mary football passes which 5-13 can also do better than any human =
quarterback,=20
using its peripheral devices). Xulon Press could be there to video this =
event as=20
GODBOT uses a peripheral add-on arm (like the Canada Arm?) to fire a =
football=20
all the way across campus. They can put this historic event out to the =
whole=20
wide world on Xulon's "God Tube" daily messages. The "God Tube" as a =
24/7=20
autoresponding machine is in effect a GODBOT already. GODBOT is another =
sign of=20
the times.</FONT></DIV>
<DIV><FONT size=3D2 face=3DArial></FONT> </DIV>
<DIV><FONT size=3D2 face=3DArial>Professor Hawking at Cambridge is the =
world's only=20
academic celebrity. He would be recognized by college students =
from Korea=20
to Kenya.<STRONG><U> Oxford would certainly give Hawkingbot a higher =
score as=20
applicant for a position of =E2=80=9Cgeneral-all-round-teacher=E2=80=9D =

over=20
Hawking.</U></STRONG> Why not then generate an
"astronaut robot" from <A =

href=3D"http://www.lely.com/" shape=3Drect
rel=3Dnofollow=20
target=3D_blank>http://www.lely.com</A> which has a
prominent presence =
in BC,=20
assembled to look exactly like Hawking? Hawkingbot as
5-13 can also milk =
cows=20
far better than the real Professor Hawking. Lely cow-
milking robots are =
the=20
leading marketed product for that global high tech firm
but they do far =
more=20
than milk cows. They gather and dispense knowledge and
in that sense =
they=20
practice epistemology. Presently there is no high
demand for cow milkers =
in=20
space though a Canadian Moon Colony at the Moon's
Mountain of Eternal =
Light=20
could sustain a troglodyte bovine population. But there
will be a high =
demand=20
for knowledge gathering and dispensing robots in
general when Musk et al =

colonize Moon, Mars and start mining asteroids in space,
all of which =
they will=20
do by the time Canadian babies born now are young
adults. This is =
another reason=20
why Senate and and all four parties of the House of
Commons cc'd with =
this=20
letter should welcome 5-13 during Question Period. How
would Canadian=20
civilization itself be described if it were exported to
British Columbia =
and=20

then to a Canadian Lunar Colony? Musk, Branson and other space-farers =
among the=20
young billionaire leaders of this planet are asking similar questions =
now. How=20
shall we live in space? A Canadian Catechism generated by =
parliamentarians for=20
GODBOT can tell the world.</FONT></DIV>
<DIV><FONT size=3D2 face=3DArial></FONT> </DIV>
<DIV><FONT size=3D2 face=3DArial>ASK THE
EXPERTS!</FONT></DIV>
<DIV><FONT size=3D2 face=3DArial></FONT> </DIV>
<DIV><FONT size=3D2 face=3DArial><STRONG><U>CHAPTER 1:
</U>CANADA'S =
QUESTION=20
PERIOD</STRONG></FONT></DIV>
<DIV><FONT size=3D2 face=3DArial></FONT> </DIV>
<DIV><FONT face=3DArial></FONT> </DIV>
<DIV><FONT size=3D2 face=3DArial><STRONG><FONT
color=3D#ff0000 =
size=3D3>Where wast thou=20
when I laid the foundations of the
Earth?</FONT></STRONG> - Job=20
38:4</FONT></DIV>
<DIV><FONT size=3D2 face=3DArial></FONT> </DIV>
<DIV><FONT size=3D2 face=3DArial>It is unfortunate that
Prime Minister =
Chretien and=20
MP Robinson did not carry on with their disagreement about defining the =
God of=20
the Canadian Constitution during Question Period. But Robot 5-13 can do =
this. It=20
can educate the world 24/7 without any need for sleep, feeding or other =
breaks.=20
In doing so, it opens up the way for explaining to Canadians what the =
entire=20
Constitution of Canada really means. Let us call this opening up of =
Question=20
Periods our "Patriot Act". Another wise saying of Prime Minister =

Chretien's was=20
"The Constitution belongs to the people". GODBOT can open up an Internet =
line to=20
all 35,000,000 present Canadians. Aristotle said "If liberty and =
equality, as is=20
thought by some, are chiefly to be found in democracy, they will be best =

attained when all persons alike share in the government to the utmost". =
It is=20
unfortunate that the now-defunct Reform Party did not take on the =
responsibility=20
to lead the small group involvements at the constituency level which =
would have=20
been necessary for Aristotelean politics to succeed. Even Sociology 100 =
tells us=20
the organizing and leadership which starts with a constituency of about =
100,000=20
having an MP must descend to the grass roots level. For example "10" =
could be=20
the unit of political organizing. 10 -> 100 -> 1,000 -> 10,000 =
->=20
100,000. "Reform" was doomed to failure even before it elected one of =
its many=20
MPs. Question Period would have had to reach the grass roots level for =
it to=20
succeed. How would the three wise men of the west, Socrates, Plato and=20
Aristotle, use =E2=80=9CSocratic Dialogue=E2=80=9D to program GODBOT =
compared to the three wise=20
men from the east in the Gospel Story? Are there any philosophers with =
expertise=20
in Socratic methods who can answer that?</FONT></DIV>
<DIV><FONT size=3D2 face=3DArial></FONT> </DIV>

```
<DIV><FONT size=3D2 face=3DArial>A Cambridge 5-13 robot
according to job =
description=20
must teach epistemology and metaphysics. Epistemology
has to do with =
knowledge=20
in general. Let us then start the 5-13 grammatical
program in C computer =

language grammar with the KNOWLEDGE OF METAPHYSICS.
What could be more =
general=20
than metaphysics which is above, beyond ... on top of
the whole wide=20
world?  Metaphysics has to do with transcendence
or ineffability =
Job 38:4=20
is an example. If those =E2=80=9Cfoundations=E2=80=9D
refer to a Big =
Bang-like event, there is=20
no time/place in our terms which precedes it. Job 38:4
is ineffable. And =
now,=20
for the first time in history, ineffability has come
into the science =
lab via=20
quantum studies. Poetically, in the popular song lyrics
of The=20
Carpenters:</FONT></DIV>
<DIV><FONT size=3D2 face=3DArial></FONT> </DIV>
<DIV><FONT size=3D2 face=3DArial>I'm on top of the
world, looking down =
on=20
creation;</FONT></DIV>
<DIV><FONT size=3D2 face=3DArial>And the only
explanation I can find, is =
the love=20
that I found, ever since You've been
around,</FONT></DIV>
<DIV><FONT size=3D2 face=3DArial>Your love's put me on
the top of the=20
world.</FONT></DIV>
<DIV><FONT size=3D2 face=3DArial></FONT> </DIV>
<DIV><FONT size=3D2 face=3DArial>The books of the Bible
are recognized =
by billions=20
of Jews, Catholics, Protestants and Christians who are
```

not Catholics or=20
Protestants as well as Muslims and others (even some
Buddhists and =
Hindus) as=20
carrying <STRONG><U>an amazing revelation of
metaphysics</U></STRONG>. =
This=20
revelation comes in the form of grammatical First
Person words from God =
which=20
some Bibles set out in Red Letters. Red Letter words
have a grammatical =
form=20
which is in essence, I am God and I say ________________.
These are put =
forward=20
in print as the direct words of God in contrast with
indirect black =
letter words=20
which are commentary on the direct words and deeds of
God. Words however =
do not=20
suffice to express how awesome this Biblical claim is
and it is an =
awesome claim=20
even to those who reject the validity of the words. The
claim is=20
this:</FONT></DIV>
<DIV><FONT size=3D2 face=3DArial></FONT> </DIV>
<DIV><FONT size=3D2=20
face=3DArial>***
******************=
****
*****************=
****
*****************=
****
**</FONT></DIV>
<DIV><FONT size=3D2 face=3DArial><STRONG>God, who is
ineffable by =
definition and=20
transcends all creation including the creation of words
and the creation =
of=20
billions of galaxies x billions of stars has
occasionally spoken =
directly to=20

people on this planet</STRONG>.</FONT></DIV>
<DIV><FONT size=3D2=20
face=3DArial>*************************************
*****************=
****
*******************=
****
*******************=
****
**</FONT></DIV>
<DIV><FONT size=3D2 face=3DArial></FONT> </DIV>
<DIV><FONT size=3D2 face=3DArial>Metaphysics by bare
bones definition =
does not have=20
to be personal. The metaphysical realm does not have to
be populated. =
However=20
the <U>sacred tradition of the Hebrew people</U> was
that the Almighty =
is=20
metaphysical but could also be physically manifested.
He could speak =
through and=20
even become a flesh-and-blood or other physically
incarnated=20
manifestation. God speaks to Job and his friends
through the =
whirlwind.=20
God speaks to Moses "out of the mountain" (Exodus 19:3).
In Exodus 20:21 =
Moses=20
nears the "thick darkness" which is "where God was". In
Exodus 3:2 the =
"Angel of=20
the Lord" appeared to Moses "in a flame of fire" which
is "in the midst =
of the=20
thorn bush". Since we read in Exodus 3:4 that God CALLS
to Moses out of =
the=20
midst of the thorn bush, either the Angel of the Lord
is God the Holy =
Spirit or=20
a lesser angel and given the grammar it is reasonable
to understand this =
as God=20
the Holy Spirit. </FONT><FONT size=3D2

face=3DArial>That is how Moses =
understood his=20
Red Letter, audible-verbal encounters with God
though God says in =
Exodus=20
33:20 "You cannot see My face". In Exodus 33:9-10 we
read that "the =
cloudy=20
pillar descended and stood at the door of the
tabernacle". God spoke =
with Moses=20
and "all the people saw the cloudy pillar". In the last
chapter of =
Exodus (38)=20
we read that the cloud was upon the tabernacle by day
and the fire by =
night were=20
in the sight of ALL the House of Israel. When the cloud
was taken up the =
Hebrew=20
nomads journeyed on. All means 600,000 according to
"Essential Judaism: =
A=20
Complete Guide to Beliefs, Customs, and Rituals" (page
431) by George =
Robinson.=20
The pillar cloud was specifically seen by Aaron,
brother of Moses and =
his wife=20
Miriam in Numbers 12:5 where we read that the Lord came
down in that =
cloud -that=20
means He was physically manifested to human beings
through the cloud. =
Sometimes=20
God is said to be present IN these physical objects and
sometimes the =
objects=20
are signs ASSOCIATED with His presence. The carnal
(flesh and blood)=20
manifestation of God is indicated in other passages.
</FONT><FONT =
size=3D2=20
face=3DArial>Who was the MAN worshipped by Joshua as
God in Joshua =
5:13-15? Who=20
was the MAN who wrestled with Jacob in Genesis 32:24,

who then blessed =
Jacob and=20
gave him the new name and title of Israel whereby he is
said to have =
power with=20
both God and humankind? </FONT><FONT size=3D2
face=3DArial>This thread =
of God being=20
the ineffable God (purely metaphysical or purely
spiritual) and also =
manifested=20
as Man is very clear in the Old Testament and it is
carried forward to =
New=20
Testament. Experts in religion use such passages to
find support for New =

Testament Holy Trinity teaching in the Old Testament.
Experts in quantum =
science=20
will see the analogy in quantum science where A can be
both A and not-A =
at the=20
same time. This is elaborated in the Rock Hunter book,
"The Jew Who Said =
He Was=20
God" (TJWSHWG). </FONT></DIV>
<DIV> </DIV>
<DIV><FONT size=3D2 face=3DArial>It is likewise
according to the =
<U>sacred teaching=20
authority of the Hebrew people</U> which may be oral or
written that God =
who is=20
spirit was also physically manifested in various ways
as above. The =
primary=20
reference for teaching and tradition is <U>sacred
scripture</U> so these =

are</FONT><FONT size=3D2 face=3DArial> the three inter-
related pillars =
on which=20
Judaism stands: sacred tradition, sacred teaching and
sacred scripture. =
But=20
"Judaism has never called for an unreasoning faith" we

read in the De =
Sola Poole=20
Traditional Jewish Prayer Book and Jews of all
denominations could be =
expected=20
to be very receptive to questions and answers through
GODBOT. "Judaism =
is one=20
... denominations are many" (Jewish Almanac, 1980, page
504). On the =
other hand=20
blind dogmatists, bigots and fanatics are anathema to
good, honest =
questions.<U>=20
What competent religionist would not welcome questions
about the Red =
Letter God=20
of the Bible?</U> How will MPs and Senators relate to
GODBOT on =
Parliament Hill=20
during Question Period? It needs repeating that GODBOT
is programmed =
with a=20
series of ESPs (Expert System Programs) put in place by
experts and =
these are=20
followed by Q-A sets, also prepared by experts.
<STRONG><U>The present =
writing=20
is only a treatise on the grammatical framework for
GODBOT</U></STRONG>. =
Any and=20
all particulars are left to experts. GODBOT is the
space age electronic =
blank=20
page on which the experts can write their political-
religious catechisms =
(highly=20
authoritative works). The present writing does not put
material on those =

pages.</FONT></DIV>
<DIV><FONT size=3D2 face=3DArial></FONT> </DIV>
<DIV><FONT size=3D2 face=3DArial>A number of Red Letter
question and =
answer (Q-A)=20
sets are found in the Bible. Those who see the Hebrew

Bible as sacred =
scripture=20
will understand this well. Abraham questions God about
the destruction =
of Sodom=20
and Gomorrah in Genesis Chapter 18. Joshua asks God if
He is for the =
Israelites=20
or their foes (Joshua 5:13). Gideon asks this
question and others =
in=20
Judges 6:13. God questions Job and his friends about
the limitations of =
their=20
knowledge ... human knowledge. David questions God
about his battle with =
the=20
Philistines in I Chronicles Chapter 14; also I Samuel
23:2 and 30:8. God =
answers=20
clearly. TJWSHWG engaged in various New Testament Q-A
sessions. =
Reasoning and=20
proof/testing are very much a Biblical mainstay and
critics who claim =
the Bible=20
is irrational should read more closely. In Red Letters
we read "Let us =
reason=20
together" (Isaiah 1:18) and in black letter commentary,
"Prove all =
things" (I=20
Thess. 5:21). It is hard to imagine arriving at proof
of a case by =
reason in any=20
court, secular or religious without questions and
answers. What then is =
the=20
argument against programming GODBOT as a highly
authoritative teaching =
machine=20
for many subjects? It cannot be any more heretical to
install those =
words in=20
GODBOT than to install them in a Xulon You Tube or
print publication; or =
to=20

present them by various high technology means in the
God Quad at Notre=20
Dame.</FONT></DIV>
<DIV><FONT size=3D2 face=3DArial></FONT> </DIV>
<DIV><FONT size=3D2 face=3DArial>ASK THE
EXPERTS!</FONT></DIV>
<DIV><FONT size=3D2 face=3DArial></FONT> </DIV>
<DIV><FONT size=3D2 face=3DArial><STRONG><U>CHAPTER 2:
</U>C FOR=20
CANADIAN?</STRONG></FONT></DIV>
<DIV><FONT size=3D2 face=3DArial></FONT> </DIV>
<DIV><FONT size=3D2 face=3DArial><STRONG><FONT
color=3D#ff0000 =
size=3D3>Is it not for=20
you to know judgement? Who hate the good and love the =
evil</FONT></STRONG> ....=20
- Micah 3:2-3</FONT></DIV>
<DIV><FONT size=3D2 face=3DArial></FONT> </DIV>
<DIV><FONT size=3D2 face=3DArial>The late Prime
Minister Trudeau chose =
justice and=20
the "Just Society" as his banner. He closes his chapter
in "Toward A =
Just=20
Society" (1990) with a poetic and metaphysical
expression. We read that =
"our=20
Great Helmsman is indeed steering Canada toward peace
and reconciliation =
- the=20
kind to be found in the graveyards of the deep" (page
385). =
Perhaps he=20
foresaw the imminent and inevitable balkanization of
Canada. Yet every =
end is a=20
new beginning.</FONT></DIV>
<DIV><FONT size=3D2 face=3DArial></FONT> </DIV>
<DIV><FONT size=3D2 face=3DArial>Any computing or
machine language is a =
grammar and=20
prima facie it is as value-neutral as a blank piece of
paper. It does =
not=20
advocate any ideology, religion, doctrine or belief
system. That is the=20
responsibility of experts in the related fields. An AI

like 5-13 has a =
tabula=20
rasa machine "brain" upon which anything can be written. That should =
appeal to=20
Parliamentarians who champion equality rights in Charter section 15. =
S.15 does=20
not however deny anyone the opportunity to prove ideological =
superiority. S.15=20
is like the starting gate in a horse race. It gives all an equal chance =
in the=20
race but not an equal chance to win.</FONT></DIV>
<DIV><FONT size=3D2 face=3DArial></FONT> </DIV>
<DIV><FONT size=3D2 face=3DArial>To program robot 5-13 with Red Letter=20
monologue-lectures from Genesis to Revelation is easy. In fact all of C=20
programming and other computer programming is easy. High technology =
people seem=20
to work hard at keeping this knowledge from the public. The present =
GODBOT=20
treatise makes the point that educational robotics will soon put an end =
to=20
exploitation of the uneducated as we see in popularized computing. =
But the=20
general plan is also found in various Yahoo lists as in the cc field of =
this=20
"Love Letter to Parliament": example, C-and-SEE. Computer languages are =
complex=20
but easy just as a chess C program is complex and easy (easily applied). =
With a=20
sufficiently powerful computer brain, 5-13 will not lose a chess game to =
anyone.=20
With ease it defeats all adversaries. With the correct C program, =
written by=20

experts it can answer questions about Red Letter
metaphysics better than =
any=20
single human expert when it is programmed by many
experts and by the =
best of=20
those experts ... the best of the best. As Hawking's
robotic twin it =
will teach=20
math-physics better than Hawking. Why then would
sensible and thrifty =
students=20
not enroll in a 5-13 class at minimal cost rather than
an expensive =
Hawking=20
class?</FONT></DIV>
<DIV><FONT size=3D2 face=3DArial></FONT> </DIV>
<DIV><FONT size=3D2 face=3DArial>Consider C as a
grammar which can be =
used=20
(responded to as if understood) by the machine. The
units of this =
grammar are=20
called functions by Prata in his 2002 text, C Primer
Plus. On page 301 =
he says=20
"C's design philosophy is to use functions as building
blocks" and "A =
function=20
is a self-contained unit of program code designed to
accomplish a =
particular=20
task". In other words, C grammar is a language of the
machine which =
tells the=20
machine what to do. Pertainiing to the present task of
5-13, Prata =
writes "For=20
example, printf() causes data to be printed on your
screen". The =
particular=20
characters required to use printf() can be asked of any
C expert or =
located in a=20
text like Prata's. A print statement in C can be used
to encapsulate any =

monologue/lecture. Off-the-shelf software can be
installed to have 5-13 =
turn the=20
print into oral expression as Hawking's voice
synthesizer does. =
</FONT></DIV>
<DIV><FONT size=3D2 face=3DArial></FONT> </DIV>
<DIV><FONT size=3D2 face=3DArial>The standard
educational procedure =
entails a=20
monologue/lecture followed by Q-A sessions with
students. Law makers =
proceed the=20
same way with legislation, executive decisions and
other matters of =
importance=20
to public administration followed by Question
Period.</FONT></DIV>
<DIV><FONT size=3D2 face=3DArial>After printf()
delivers the lecture, =
another=20
function can be used so that 5-13 does the opposite.
Instead of an =
output of=20
words (more broadly, characters) it inputs the audience
or student =
questions.=20
The functions necessary for this are found in Prata's
Chapter 4 titled=20
"Character Strings and Formatted Input/Output" as well
as other =
chapters. C's=20
grammatical functions can instruct 5-13 to read print
as well as type =
print.=20
Student questions can be presented through off-the-
shelf software which =
turns=20
oral questioning into print. After that, functions like
getchar() will =
input=20
characters/words of student questions to 5-13 so that
it can respond =
with=20
answers.</FONT></DIV>
<DIV><FONT size=3D2 face=3DArial></FONT> </DIV>
<DIV><FONT size=3D2 face=3DArial>Programmers will carry

on with the =
"design=20
philosophy" (to use Prata's expression) for 5-13 as an
epistemological =
machine=20
which is amenable to all questions and answers of
interest to =
parliamentarians=20
in Canada and beyond.</FONT></DIV>
<DIV><FONT size=3D2 face=3DArial></FONT> </DIV>
<DIV><FONT size=3D2 face=3DArial>ASK THE
EXPERTS!</FONT></DIV>
<DIV><FONT size=3D2 face=3DArial></FONT> </DIV>
<DIV><FONT size=3D2 face=3DArial><STRONG><U>CHAPTER
3: </U>A =
CANADIAN=20
RENAISSANCE</STRONG></FONT></DIV>
<DIV><FONT size=3D2 face=3DArial></FONT> </DIV>
<DIV><FONT size=3D2 face=3DArial><STRONG><FONT
color=3D#ff0000 =
size=3D3>Art thou=20
(Nicodemus) a master of Israel and<FONT color=3D#ff0000>
knowest =
</FONT>not these=20
things?</FONT></STRONG> - John 3:10</FONT></DIV>
<DIV><FONT size=3D2 face=3DArial></FONT> </DIV>
<DIV><FONT size=3D2 face=3DArial>In the passage above,
TJWSHWG is =
speaking to a=20
Jewish Pharisee leader who recognizes Jesus as a
"rabbi", a "a teacher =
come from=20
God" because of the miracles (John 3:2) but Nicodemus
had yet to =
recognize the=20
miracle of renaissance which is rebirth. A Canadian
Renaissance, defined =
as a=20
rebirth of civilization is imminent. When we consider
how Canadians =
might live=20
on the Moon over the next few decades we will
inevitably reconsider how =
they=20
live here.</FONT></DIV>
<DIV><FONT size=3D2 face=3DArial></FONT> </DIV>
<DIV><FONT size=3D2 face=3DArial>The first Red Letter

words of the Bible =
are "Let=20
there be light". These four words may be accompanied in
a C program with =

corresponding black letter commentary. After that
lecture, there will be =
student=20
questions. It is the human experts who will initially
answer those =
questions.=20
Their answers are then programmed into 5-13 by C
programmers who may use =
C "if=20
statements". In Prata (page 221) we read, "The if
statement is called a=20
branching statement or selection statement because it
provides a =
junction where=20
the program has to select which of two paths to
follow".The general form =
given=20
is</FONT></DIV>
<DIV><FONT size=3D2 face=3DArial></FONT> </DIV>
<DIV><FONT size=3D2 face=3DArial>if
(expression)</FONT></DIV>
<DIV><FONT size=3D2 =
face=3DArial>
 =20
statement </FONT></DIV>
<DIV><FONT size=3D2 face=3DArial></FONT> </DIV>
<DIV><FONT size=3D2 face=3DArial>If students ask a
certain question =
pertaining to=20
the fiat lux lecture such as "What is light?" then 5-13
will respond =
___________=20
where the blank is filled in by human experts.
Experienced college =
lecturers=20
will say that after giving a course so many times, they
are rarely =
surprised by=20
a new student question. "What is light?" and similar
questions will be =
grouped=20
and any variation in that group will evoke the same

answer from GODBOT.=20
Questions of this nature will lead to answers about literal and =
metaphorical=20
uses of the word light. Literal questions may even deal with the physics =
of=20
light. Why does e =3D mc2 and not mc3? Where is there a nuclear reactor =
anywhere=20
on this planet with data to answer the question? If they are not =
forthcoming=20
with the information, why is that?</FONT></DIV>
<DIV><FONT size=3D2 face=3DArial></FONT> </DIV>
<DIV><FONT size=3D2 face=3DArial>The programming technology for Q-A =
sessions is the=20
same as that used by Google and other search engines. The =
words/characters we=20
insert into the search engine are essentially questions. Two words: =
"question"=20
and "period", give similar results or answers to the question "What is =
Question=20
Period?" But the important difference for educational purposes has to do =
with=20
"human equivalency". <STRONG><U>Since 5-13 (aka GODBOT or Hawkingbot) as =
a=20
Hawking-lookalike is performing like the real Hawking lecturer, it will =
be=20
accepted by students whereas non-humanoid teaching machines are not=20
accepted</U></STRONG>. Moreover, thousands of subjects can be taught =
this way=20
and at very low cost. (Read again the trillion dollar student debt above =
- and=20
that is US only). The initial cost of C programming is mostly related to =

grouping the questions after each lecture and linking
them by if-then =
code as=20
above to the best answers. Given the success of pro
bono public =
education=20
through wiki and related projects, one would expect
many volunteer =
experts to=20
come forward and provide this assistance. Thousands of
sets of course =
materials=20
gathered from hundreds of universities by MIT since
2001 in a project =
called OCW=20
(Open Courseware) have no value unless they are taught.
They can be =
taught by=20
5-13.</FONT></DIV>
<DIV><FONT size=3D2 face=3DArial></FONT> </DIV>
<DIV><FONT size=3D2 face=3DArial>The metaphysics lesson
on light becomes =
an=20
educational enlightenment in the broadest sense. The
Cambridge job =
description=20
requires teaching of epistemology as well as
metaphysics. Since 5-13 can =
teach=20
knowledge in thousands of subjects, it meets that
requirement. It is a=20
metaphysics-epistemology-teaching robot, a God Tube
robot and it sets a =
"new=20
direction in (artificial) mind" which is also part of
the Cambridge job=20
description. If Cambridge does not want to hire
Hawkingbot, perhaps =
Oxford does.=20
The English who led the Industrial Revolution must be
tempted to lead =
the Robot=20
Revolution.</FONT></DIV>
<DIV><FONT size=3D2 face=3DArial></FONT> </DIV>
<DIV><FONT size=3D2 face=3DArial>ASK THE
EXPERTS!</FONT></DIV>
<DIV><FONT size=3D2 face=3DArial></FONT> </DIV>

<DIV><FONT size=3D2 face=3DArial><STRONG><U>CHAPTER 4:
</U>RED LETTER =
CANADIAN=20
PRINCIPLES</STRONG></FONT></DIV>
<DIV><FONT size=3D2 face=3DArial></FONT> </DIV>
<DIV><FONT size=3D2 face=3DArial><STRONG><FONT
color=3D#ff0000 =
size=3D3>Come now, and=20
let us reason together ... though your sins be as
scarlet, they shall be =
as=20
white as snow</FONT></STRONG> - Isaiah=20
1:18   &nb
sp;   &nb=
sp;   &nbs
p;   &nbs=
p; =20
</FONT></DIV>
<DIV><FONT size=3D2 face=3DArial></FONT> </DIV>
<DIV><FONT size=3D2 face=3DArial>The three pillars
of Israelite =
faith are=20
presented in Chapter 1. Before the Israelites were
given the sacred =
teaching=20
authority of the Decalogue or Ten Commandments they
lived under Egyptian =

dominion without this revelation. During those
centuries, the population =

expanded from the extended family of Jacob (Israel) to
600,000 migrating =
people=20
at Mount Sinai. Sacred teaching was associated with
supporting sacred =
traditions=20
(customs, rituals, rites etc) and sacred writings ...
the Bible. =
Robinson says=20
"The Bible is a book with many names, as befits a work
that is protean =
in form=20
and cosmic in scope" (page 257). He refers to it as the
"Hebrew Bible" =
listing=20
its 39 booklets from Genesis to II Chronicles on pages

258-259. Robinson =
does=20
not recognize the New Testament booklets like the book
titled "Hebrews". =
One=20
might ask his religious authorities to reason out what
is objectionable =
about=20
Hebrews? Why does it not describe the perfect Hebrew
sacrifice ... the =
perfect=20
and unforgettable offering?</FONT></DIV>
<DIV><FONT size=3D2 face=3DArial></FONT> </DIV>
<DIV><FONT size=3D2 face=3DArial>Sacred
writings/teachings are passed on =
over=20
hundreds and thousands of years and they constitute
sacred tradition of=20
themselves along with associated acts. They may be
passed on =
ritualistically and=20
with ceremony as part of other sacred traditions. The
Decalogue is =
supported by=20
all three sacred pillars. Israelite teaching
authorities must therefore =
be very=20
upset by any diminution, alteration or desecration of
the Ten =
Commandments.=20
Parliament serves a Constitution which is "founded upon
principles" as =
we read=20
in the Canadian Charter of Rights and Freedoms.
</FONT><FONT size=3D2=20
face=3DArial>The Ten Commandments pertain to TEN
important principles. =
Each is=20
distinct and very clearly and easily differentiated
from any other. They =
cannot=20
be fused together or conflated, nor can any one be
artificially split up =
or=20
dissembled. They can of course be summarized as the
general title =
(Decalogue or=20

Ten Commandments) is a summarization.</FONT></DIV>
<DIV><FONT size=3D2 face=3DArial></FONT> </DIV>
<DIV><FONT size=3D2 face=3DArial>Given that the courts of Canada have =
defined the=20
"supremacy of God clause" in our Constitution as Canadian highest =
principles,=20
the TEN PRINCIPLES of the Ten Commandments must be of great interest to=20
law-makers. They must also ask what the so-called "Traditional =
Catechetical=20
Formula" for the Decalogue does to its meaning. Refer to paragraphs =
2051-2052 of=20
Catechism of the Catholic Church, Pope John Paul II (Karl Josef Wojtyla) =

edition. The First Commandment of the traditional (and sacred) Israelite =

phrasing is fused with the second, rendering them one command. This=20
fusion/conflation creates confusion. The God of the Hebrews is not an =
author of=20
confusion (a question per se is not a confusion). The sacred Israelite =
First=20
Commandment is analogous to an "Order in the Court" proclamation. But =
this=20
Commandment does infinitely more. It commands and demands that the =
metaphysical=20
realm be recognized as more than a universal or mother nature machine. =
The=20
universe has a PERSONAL CREATOR. Canadians of course are free by law to =
disagree=20
with that. The Second Command or Principle is that "You shall have no =
other gods=20
before me". It is clearly not the same as the First. With equal =

confusion, the=20
Traditional Catechetical Formula takes the Tenth
Commandment "Thou shalt =
not=20
covet _______" and turns it into two separate commands
by giving two =
examples of=20
covetousness. That becomes extremely questionable also
by elementary =
logic. If=20
two examples create two Commandments, why are there not
200 or 2,000=20
Commandments? Of course the Bible carries many orders
and directives =
from God.=20
But there are only TEN primary Commandments which can
be SUMMARIZED (not =

conflated or dissembled) in the Summary of the Law. The
Baptist =
"Traditional=20
Catechetical Formula" is also available online and it
too rephrases the=20
Decalogue in ways which detract from its clear and
distinct ten=20
principles.</FONT></DIV>
<DIV><FONT size=3D2 face=3DArial></FONT> </DIV>
<DIV><FONT size=3D2 face=3DArial>What do Ten Principles
have to do with =
Question=20
Period? EVERYTHING. "Canada is founded upon principles
that recognize =
the=20
supremacy of God". Perhaps that is the deeper cause of
Nielsen's =
polemical book:=20
He writes as if he was denied the right or power or
opportunity to ask =
good,=20
honest questions about those fundamental principles of
Canadian =
civilization ...=20
the principles that Canadians would want to export to
secessionist BC =
and from=20
there to the Moon as BC First Nations prepare to
uncouple BC from =

Canada.=20
</FONT><FONT size=3D2 face=3DArial>As parliamentarians write the new =
Catechism of=20
Canada for those "highest principles" in a model civilization located in =
BC what=20
will it be like? How will it read? This is a huge responsibility for=20
parliamentary experts. Since any political-religious catechism presents =
itself=20
as HIGHLY authoritative, <STRONG><U>the entire presentation becomes =
suspect when=20
a major untruth is discovered.
</U></STRONG></FONT></DIV>
<DIV><FONT size=3D2 =
face=3DArial><STRONG><U></U></STRONG></FONT> </DIV>
<DIV><FONT size=3D2 face=3DArial>Robson refers to "The Almighty" =
repeatedly in his=20
book and recognizes the many names for The Almighty. The word Almighty =
means=20
all-powerful. An all-powerful Deity by definition has all power over =
knowledge=20
and ignorance; all power over perfection and imperfection; all power =
over good=20
and evil. Traditions, even sacred traditions, do indeed change. The =
"Golden Calf=20
Rebellion" was crushed by the Israelite authorities who were led by =
Moses with=20
support of his Levite clan. They slaughtered thousands of fellow=20
Israelites for violating the Second Commandment. It is difficult to =
imagine=20
modern Israel doing this when Prime Minister Golda Meier once lamented =
the=20
problem of national cohesiveness in a nation with one third Atheist =

believers.=20
Atheism rejects the First Commandment. Moses would not have spared the =
life of=20
anyone calling him or God a liar as Atheistic Jews do. Perhaps by =
recognizing=20
the change in sacred traditions over the centuries we can explain Roman=20
Catholicism's catechetical deviation from the sacred tradition of the =
Israelite=20
teaching authority. In what century was this new Decalogue "formula" =
invented?=20
What other questionable statements, questionable formulas and untruths =
might one=20
find in Catholic Catechism or the Protestant Catechisms? When did =
Israelite=20
civiilzation recognize Atheism as a valid Israelite belief system? When =
did it=20
start to deny the teachings of TJWSHWG as the Israelite way forward when =
the New=20
Testament Bible refers repeatedly to followers of TJWSHWG as=20
Israelites/Judahites and Jews and only three times as =
"Christians"?</FONT></DIV>
<DIV><FONT size=3D2 face=3DArial></FONT> </DIV>
<DIV><FONT size=3D2 face=3DArial>So many questions arise when good, =
honest,=20
principled people discuss principles. Fortunately there are experts to =
answer=20
which rules out bigots (the dead who bury the dead) and blind dogmatists =
(the=20
blind who lead the blind). Experts in the principles of God are not =
prejudiced=20
people who pre-judge the statements of others and call them heretical =
without=20

justification. The Question Period of Parliament
according to GODBOT's=20
catechetical formula becomes a political-religious
activity. How could =
it be=20
otherwise? Highest principles are highest principles no
matter who puts =
them=20
forward and no matter what their vocation.</FONT></DIV>
<DIV><FONT size=3D2 face=3DArial></FONT> </DIV>
<DIV><FONT size=3D2 face=3DArial>ASK THE
EXPERTS!</FONT></DIV>
<DIV><FONT size=3D2 face=3DArial></FONT> </DIV>
<DIV><FONT size=3D2 face=3DArial><STRONG><U>CHAPTER 5:
</U>PEACE, ORDER =
AND GOOD=20
CANADIAN GOVERNMENT</STRONG></FONT></DIV>
<DIV><FONT size=3D2 face=3DArial></FONT> </DIV>
<DIV><FONT size=3D2 face=3DArial></FONT> </DIV>
<DIV><FONT size=3D2 face=3DArial><FONT color=3D#ff0000
=
size=3D3><STRONG>Be still and=20
know that I am God</STRONG></FONT> - Psalms
46:10</FONT></DIV>
<DIV><FONT size=3D2 face=3DArial></FONT> </DIV>
<DIV><FONT size=3D2 face=3DArial>The Red Letter
expression above sounds =
like a Hindu=20
or Zen Buddhist mantra (which instructs the stilling of
the mind). The=20
monotheistic teachings of the patriarchs in Babylon
preceded Hinduism =
and=20
Buddhism as well as the religions of Ancient China.
Absolute knowledge =
came to=20
Elijah, not in the great wind or the rocks or
earthquake or fire but in =
"a=20
still, small voice" (I Kings 19:12) and that still,
small voice of God =
posed a=20
question to Elijah, "What are you doing here?" The
great swelling words =
and=20
words as shallow as sounding brass (Biblical
expressions) which emanate =

from=20
political-religious frauds do not answer that simple and sound question =
from=20
God. What are parliamentarians doing here? What are millions of popes, =
priests=20
and preachers doing here? What are typical Canadians doing here and can =
we do=20
better by designing a CANOPOLIS well?</FONT></DIV>
<DIV><FONT size=3D2 face=3DArial></FONT> </DIV>
<DIV><FONT size=3D2 face=3DArial>The phrase "peace, order and good =
government" can=20
be accessed by www search and is often used in parliamentary systems. =
Who are=20
the experts in spelling out the meaning of "good" as a comprehensive way =
of life=20
... a civilization, for this planet and beyond? Though an Almighty God =
by=20
definition (and by reality to believers) has full power over all good =
and evil,=20
the Bible is clear and consistent in Red Letter directives and black =
letter=20
commentary that man is to choose good. Red Letters state clearly in Amos =
5:15=20
"Hate the evil, and love the good_____". Red Letters ask Solomon =
to make a=20
request. In I Kings 3:5, Solomon asks "<STRONG><U>to discern between =
good and=20
bad"</U></STRONG> and his wish is granted. Popular knowledge is "the =
wisdom of=20
Solomon". But Biblical passages subordinate wisdom to "love the good" =
and for=20
believers that must lead to God as the creator of all that is good. We =

read that=20
the wisdom of man is foolishness to God. Solomon also
did not ask for=20
righteousness as we read that there is none righteous,
no not one. What =
then do=20
we say of those who claim to be holy or pious in their
righteousness? =
Hollywood=20
has no difficulty finding actors to play the roles of
religionists who =
make such=20
claims for themselves. Solomon's request sounds as
simple as a child's =
Christmas=20
wish. But it was honest and sound and it was granted.
That was the =
wisdom of=20
Solomon and one might argue that it was even on a
higher level than what =
we=20
usually call wisdom since good-bad originates
metaphysically. There is =
no=20
physical formula for good- bad.</FONT></DIV>
<DIV><FONT size=3D2 face=3DArial></FONT> </DIV>
<DIV><FONT size=3D2 face=3DArial>If we ask the religion
masters, why not =
start with=20
those who are experts in the Hebrew Bible which
presents <STRONG><U>the=20
idealization of civilization</U></STRONG> beginning
with Eden and =
continuing=20
through the centuries with the struggles of the
Israelites toward =
establishing=20
their idealized "Kingdom of God" on this planet? T.J.
Wray writes in her =
text,=20
"What The Bible Really Tells Us" (WTBRTU) that Heaven
should be =
differentiated=20
from Kingdom of Heaven or Kingdom of God. She calls the
Christian Bible =
which=20
she uses a "Hebrew Bible" which is generically correct.

All Christian =
Bibles are=20
Hebrew Bibles. The New Testament carries forward Old
Testament =
teachings. It=20
does not revoke them. We read on page 108 that
Heaven "should not =
be=20
confused with what Jesus calls the Kingdom of God,
sometimes rendered =
the=20
Kingdom of Heaven in the Gospel of Matthew, which
refers to an earthly =
reality".=20
A most important 'rendering' is in The Lord's Prayer
(the only formal =
prayer=20
given by TJWSHWG). Since billions of Christians have
prayed in The =
Lord's Prayer=20
for the establishing of a materially observable
civilization of God on =
this=20
planet, should Parliament not be bringing the experts
of Christian =
religion into=20
Parliament for Question Period and the programming of
GODBOT? Do they =
know how=20
to articulate "good" as in "good, better and best"?
Perhaps Professor =
Wray=20
(Salve Regina University) can tell us in her next text
What The Bible =
Really=20
Tells Us About The <STRONG><U>Hebrew Ideal=20
Civilization</U></STRONG>.</FONT></DIV>
<DIV><FONT size=3D2 face=3DArial></FONT> </DIV>
<DIV><FONT size=3D2 face=3DArial>Why not ask the Jews
in Canada's =
multicultural=20
mosaic to write such a script since most of the Old
Testament is about =
the=20
ongoing Red Letter communications between the Almighty
and His Chosen =
People=20

toward the objective of establishing a priestly nation of priestly =
people,=20
living IHS (In His Service) 24/7? </FONT><FONT size=3D2 face=3DArial>A =
complication=20
of this matter is presented by Asimov in his book titled "Asimov's Guide =
To The=20
Bible: The Old Testament". He says that "The united kingdom over which =
David=20
thus came to rule in 1006 BC is called Israel in the Bible, but the =
kingdom was=20
never really single. The two halves of the nation were never truly =
amalgamated"=20
(page 301). The kingdom called Judah and that called Israel each had its =
own=20
king line. They were usually in conflict and sometimes at war with one =
another.=20
Judah was populated by descendants of the sons of Jacob: Judah and =
Benjamin.=20
Israel was populated by descendants of Gad, Dan, Zebullon, Joseph and =
the other=20
sons of Jacob. Levites, as the priestly clan could live in either =
kingdom. This=20
sacred tradition of the Israelites continues today in Christendom since =
the=20
priesthood of the same Christian denomination may be located in two =
countries=20
engaged in bitter warfare. Asimov writes on page 95 that "While members =
of all=20
twelve tribes are Israelites, it is the members of the tribe of Judah =
only that=20
are, strictly speaking, Judeans or Jews". In this context the point made =

by some=20
Bible scholars that the word "Jew" was a later
introduction to the =
Bible,=20
replacing Judean or Judahite is irrelevant. In the New
Testament, a list =
can be=20
made of all references to Jew and Israelite to show
that the two words =
are used=20
interchangeably. St. Paul, aka Saul, correctly refers
to himself as "the =
Jew of=20
Tarsus" and also as an Israelite of the tribe of
Benjamin.</FONT></DIV>
<DIV><FONT size=3D2 face=3DArial></FONT> </DIV>
<DIV><FONT size=3D2 face=3DArial>A man's reach must
exceed his grasp, or =
what's a=20
heaven for said the poet Blake. In Red Letters we read
in Acts 7:49 that =
Heaven=20
is God's throne and earth is His footstool. "What house
will you build =
me?" asks=20
the Lord. And though we also read in the Red Letters of
Isaiah 55:8-9 =
that "My=20
ways are higher than your ways and My thoughts are
higher than your =
thoughts",=20
the question is not merely rhetorical. In Exodus 31:2
God tells Moses He =
has=20
"called by name Bezaleel" (Tribe of Judah) and given
Bezaleel knowledge =
in all=20
workmanship as the chief builder in the Israelite
Kingdom of God. =
Despite His=20
higher ways, God interacts with humankind in this world.
That is what =
the Bible=20
is about. As Asimov writes, "The most influential, the
most published, =
the most=20
widely read book in the history of the world is the

Bible" (page 9).=20
</FONT></DIV>
<DIV><FONT size=3D2 face=3DArial></FONT> </DIV>
<DIV><FONT size=3D2 face=3DArial>Ottawa's Parliament,
therefore, as the=20
multicultural "Parliament of Nations" has already
invited all religions =
or=20
belief systems from A-Z, Atheist to Zoroastrian, to
articulate the =
ideals of=20
their civilization. Why not spell it out for export to
Moon, Mars and =
beyond?=20
</FONT></DIV>
<DIV><FONT size=3D2 face=3DArial></FONT> </DIV>
<DIV><FONT size=3D2 face=3DArial>Parliament may want to
start by =
spelling out what=20
Canadian civilization is like for export from Ottawa to
Indian land in =
British=20
Columbia. As "Gold War: The Lost Gold Mines Of Canada's
Indians" by Rock =
Hunter=20
reminds us, BC may be unique in the Western Hemisphere.
There never was =
a=20
European colonial claim over BC and there never was an
"Indian War" =
whereby the=20
winners might claim ownership of land, paid for in
blood. The only =
colonial=20
claim came from Ottawa and it has no foundation in
international =
justice. First=20
Nations of BC can walk into the UN General Assembly any
day and take a =
seat.=20
Also they can make their claim that Ottawa has engaged
in ongoing =
genocide=20
against First Nations people across Canada, proven by
extrapolation from =
the=20
Frank Paul case and Gosselin case (Supreme Court of

Canada, 2001). =
Succintly,=20
one must ask what would have happened if Paul rather
than Gosselin had =
appeared=20
before SCC. Would Judge McLaughlin et al have said to
him as they did to =

Gosselin that Canada has no duty to protect the lives
of citizens when =
they are=20
endangered by homelessness ... and also (as they did)
that it costs too =
much for=20
such justice to prevail? Would they have said it is
"justice" to keep =
putting a=20
series of First Nation Frank Pauls into cold, wet
streets by police =
action which=20
caused Frank to die of exposure? </FONT><FONT
size=3D2 =
face=3DArial>If so,=20
that demographic differential would cause the death and
destruction of =
more=20
First Nation people than average and such a
differential/discriminatory=20
administration would be genocidal. Yet the McLaughlin
SCC declared this =
to be=20
justice. The Criminal Code of Canada pertaining to
genocide can be read =
online.=20
By bizarre and false "reasoning" McLaughlin and her
majority of 5 (v the =

minority of 4) asserted in effect that justice in
Canada would not come =
from her=20
court unless it was cheap. She said that it would cost
too much to =
provide the=20
essentials for life to the mentally ill and the native
people who, in=20
combination are the majority of the homeless in Canada.
Yet a generation =

before=20
her, homelessness was almost unknown in this country
and much more =
expensive=20
institutions housed and fed the mentally ill. Thus
McLaughlin =
effectively=20
(though probably unknowingly) made a pompous
declaration in defense of =
what=20
Hitler called "useless eaters" policy. In this case the
useless eaters =
subjected=20
to Canadian genocide rather than the Hitlerian variety
are those with =
clearly=20
defined demographics: poor and native. </FONT></DIV>
<DIV><FONT size=3D2 face=3DArial></FONT> </DIV>
<DIV><FONT size=3D2 face=3DArial>The ideal of Canadian
civilization is =
not genocidal=20
and one must wonder, parenthetically if recall of
judges like SCC judges =
would=20
solve the problem? How will that model, exported from
Ottawa to BC, deal =
with=20
homeless First Nations people? Will they be subjected
to ongoing=20
homelessness-related killing conditions in the present
differential way? =
What=20
would that civilization be like, exported to Indian
land in BC and =
thence=20
off-planet? What would a model of Jewish civilization
by comparison be =
like?=20
American civilization? Chinese civilization? China
Towns are well liked =
across=20
Canada. What would a China City (of perhaps 100,000) be
like? Here in BC =
we can=20
let 1,000 flowers of multicullturalism bloom, paid for
in gold as BC =
becomes the=20

new South Africa of precious metal mining. Refer to
"Gold War". Canadian =

civilization is not only good but the best of the best
because =
_________________.=20
Spell this out for BC, feature by feature. If it is the
best of the =
best, we=20
British Columbians can export it off-
planet.</FONT></DIV>
<DIV><FONT size=3D2 face=3DArial></FONT> </DIV>
<DIV><FONT size=3D2 face=3DArial>ASK THE
EXPERTS!</FONT></DIV>
<DIV><FONT size=3D2 face=3DArial></FONT> </DIV>
<DIV><FONT size=3D2 face=3DArial></FONT> </DIV>
<DIV><FONT size=3D2 face=3DArial><STRONG><U>CHAPTER 6:
</U>GOOD, BETTER =
AND BEST IN=20
CANADA</STRONG></FONT></DIV>
<DIV><FONT size=3D2 face=3DArial></FONT> </DIV>
<DIV><FONT size=3D2 face=3DArial><STRONG><FONT
color=3D#ff0000 =
size=3D3>Hate the evil=20
and love the good</FONT></STRONG> - Amos
5:15</FONT></DIV>
<DIV><FONT size=3D2 face=3DArial></FONT> </DIV>
<DIV><FONT size=3D2 face=3DArial>BC wants to export the
best of the best =
off-planet.=20
Earth would probably import precious metals from off-
planet British =
Columbian=20
colonies since D.K. Yeomans tells us in his book,
"Near-Earth Objects" =
(2013)=20
that a one km wide rocky asteroid contains TRILLIONS of
dollars in =
precious=20
metals. "Irons" or metallic asteroids contain more.
There are tens of =
thousands=20
of trillion dollar asteroids in surface and near
surface deposits of =
Moon sand=20
Mars where the organic regolith (overburden) to block
access does not =

exist.=20
Imagine how much mineral wealth would be discovered if BC, twice the =
area of=20
Japan and over 90% mountainous, were devoid of organic overburden. On =
Mars the=20
extreme winds blow gold, silver and platinum placer deposits into crater =
and=20
canyon traps even though the atmosphere is very thin. Also they lay bare =
the=20
bedrock as they move on to other locations. Though the atmosphere is =
very thin=20
and weak, it still yields enormous formations of sand dunes and dust =
dunes. Both=20
are easily located and surface placer deposits of gold, silver and =
platinums=20
abound. On Moon, the loose sediments of the surface are very shallow, =
enabling=20
easy geophysical penetration and mapping. Why mine the asteroids =
which are=20
loose, astrogeological sedimentary floats in space when the asteroids =
are found=20
on Moon and Mars in abundance and can be mined by mining colonies of =
former=20
Earthlings? Media should ask Senator Neufeld (former mining minister in =
BC)=20
about Canadian Moon and Mars mining. Ask a good, honest question of a =
Canadian=20
in Parliament and ___________________?</FONT></DIV>
<DIV><FONT size=3D2 face=3DArial></FONT> </DIV>
<DIV><FONT size=3D2 face=3DArial>Canada does not own the land or mineral =
deposits or=20
any other natural resource of BC. Ask Senator Sibbeston this good, =

honest=20
question. But it can claim jurisdiction over present off-reservation =
personnel.=20
When those personnel are living on reservations and the social order is =
reversed=20
in that sense, applications may be made to a First Nation Space City. =
Who are=20
the "best of the best" to use a Donald Trump slogan? All of the cultures =
of=20
multiculturalism are not equal any more than all religions are equal. =
Some are=20
quite banal. Some are "terrorist" in nature. Some are evil, plain and =
simple,=20
although we tend to call these social-political-religious evils "cults" =
rather=20
than cultures. The Procult Institute of Vancouver was formed by close =
advisors=20
to former BC Premier Vanderzalm to advance the cults of Canada with its =
flagship=20
tome titled "Stop Apologizing" (1991)   by J Cyllorn. MPs in Ottawa =
at the=20
time took umbrage at Cyllorn's magnum opus. Robert Lee published in the=20
Vancouver Sun that "a number of MPs wanted J Cyllorn prosecuted for=20
hate-mongering" and that Cyllorn was "(Premier) Bill Vander Zalms's =
one-time=20
numerologist". This ceased when they realized that Madame Cyllorn still =
read the=20
tea leaf futures of Premier "Bill V", projecting numbers onto them in a =
bizarre=20
practice of superstition which once earned him the headline story of the =

Vancouver Sun daily newspaper.</FONT></DIV>
<DIV><FONT size=3D2 face=3DArial></FONT> </DIV>
<DIV><FONT size=3D2 face=3DArial>Protestants may enter the BC =
competition of=20
cultures but Protestantism is merely a branch from Catholicism. Judaic=20
Christianity on the other hand preceded both so they are branches from =
the "True=20
Vine" of the Lion of Judah. The Modern King James Version Of The Holy =
Bible by=20
Jay P. Green, Sr. goes further with its wording when it says, "Behold, =
days are=20
coming says the Lord, and I will make an end on the house of Israel, and =
on the=20
house of Judah a new covenant shall be" (Hebrews, 8:8). This wording may =
be seen=20
by some as a questionable restatement but TJWSHWG is most certainly =
described as=20
from the Judahite lineage and the final Red Letter words of the Bible =
are "I am=20
the root and the offspring of David, the bright and morning star". King =
David=20
was of course a Judahite. Thus we see an elaboration on the original C =
program=20
fiat lux lesson. Where does light (as in star light?) differ from =
literal light?=20
Is it only metaphor when Revelation refers to an angel standing in the =
light of=20
the Sun?</FONT></DIV>
<DIV><FONT size=3D2 face=3DArial></FONT> </DIV>
<DIV><FONT size=3D2 face=3DArial>What is the greatest heartfelt desire =
of humankind?=20
It people are given just one wish, what will it be? Whether it is called =

Heaven,=20
Kingdom of Heaven or Paradise, <STRONG><U>surely to
live in a state =
which=20
expresses goodness to the greatest degree, protected
forever from harm =
would sum=20
that up</U></STRONG>. That perfection would apply
within each person and =
it=20
would apply to the surroundings. Can the Pax Canadiana
provide the =
protection?=20
Prudential funded the Westlake Hills, California
development in the =
1970s and=20
used the slogan "Paradise at a Price" for advertising.
It is not merely =
utopian=20
hot air. Every developer will claim to be "doing the
best I can" whether =
the=20
project is to to expand an existing settlement or build
one totally =
anew. The=20
word "good"is central or foundational. Take it feature
by feature: =

________________ is a good feature because
__________________. We pursue =
that which=20
is good within ourselves and in our surroundings. That
formula is simple =
and=20
true.</FONT></DIV>
<DIV><FONT size=3D2 face=3DArial></FONT> </DIV>
<DIV><FONT size=3D2 face=3DArial>TJWSHWG said "Seek ye
first the Kingdom =
of Heaven".=20
With what consequence? "All these things will be added
to you". The =
experts of=20
all religions teach and preach how to live. How would
they reply to the=20
questioning of a Question Period about the model
civilization for one =
and all,=20

24/7, on and off planet? The Future Canada for babies
born now will =
include=20
off-planet habitation as an option. Therefore it is far
from vain =
imagining to=20
ask what it might be like in a BC Future city designed
now. We ask the =
experts=20
in hundreds of fields. Each of us is like the blind men
feeling =
different parts=20
of the elephant and wondering what it is. By pooling
notes, the identity =
can be=20
made. A civilization is not the project of one person.
The simple =
formula=20
becomes complex but still easily understood when
experts are required to =

communicate in standard everyday English (SEE). SEE in
hundreds or =
thousands of=20
specializations becomes a C program. The task of MPs
and Senators is to =
make=20
sure the experts translate their technical terminology
into =
SEE.</FONT></DIV>
<DIV><FONT size=3D2 face=3DArial></FONT> </DIV>
<DIV><FONT size=3D2 face=3DArial>ASK THE
EXPERTS!</FONT></DIV>
<DIV><FONT size=3D2 face=3DArial></FONT> </DIV>
<DIV><FONT size=3D2 face=3DArial><STRONG><U>CHAPTER 7:
</U>THE =
TRADITIONAL CANADIAN=20
CATECHETICAL FORMULA</STRONG></FONT></DIV>
<DIV><FONT size=3D2 face=3DArial></FONT> </DIV>
<DIV><FONT size=3D2 face=3DArial><STRONG><FONT
color=3D#ff0000 =
size=3D3>Call to me, and=20
I will answer thee, and show thee great and mighty
things which, which =
thou=20
knowest not</FONT></STRONG> - Jeremiah 33:3</FONT></DIV>
<DIV><FONT size=3D2 face=3DArial></FONT> </DIV>

<DIV><FONT size=3D2 face=3DArial>If the God of the
Canadian Constitution =
(Supremacy=20
of God Clause) is the one true God, why would the above
not apply to =
those who=20
seek His directives toward a better future for citizens
of the space age =
which=20
has just begun? In the case of this country though we
must recognize =
that we are=20
re-defining Canadianism as soon as we start to colonize
off-planet ... =
or even=20
think about it. That is how BC will be especially but
enigmatically =
helpful. To=20
explain better consider a colony of, let us say 100,000
Canadians on =
Moon or=20
Mars. They will be or become self-sufficient by
necessity. By =
generally=20
accepted space law, no nation can claim sovereignty
off-planet. But =
privacy=20
rights prevent intrusions to the colonial living space.
The inhabitants =
are=20
self-sufficient, autonomous Moonlings or Martians.
Nothing mandates that =
they=20
identify themselves as Canadians or serve Canada beyond
any commercial =
debts but=20
their Canadian origin will identify them factually as
Neo-Canadians. For =
Ottawa=20
to recognize that BC has never lawfully been part of
Canada allows =
Canadians a=20
chance to redefine themselves before exporting this
model of =
civilization at its=20
best into space.</FONT></DIV>
<DIV><FONT size=3D2 face=3DArial></FONT> </DIV>

<DIV><FONT size=3D2 face=3DArial>The Old Testament is largely a dialogue =
with=20
commentary between the Almighty God and His Chosen People. What is its=20
objective? The objective is to re-establish an idealized state of =
existence for=20
humankind on this planet. The dialogue starts with Eden and that ideal =
state. It=20
is lost when Adam and Eve yield to the temptation to know evil as well =
as good=20
which otherwise was their life 24/7. Genesis takes us through the trials =
of the=20
patriarchs after that up to Jacob/Israel. Then we have book after book =
of the=20
struggles of the Israelites with the task of re-establishing an =
idealized state,=20
a way of life for thousands or millions of people, not Adam and Eve =
alone. The=20
narrow definition of Zionism is the establishing of Israelite =
civilization=20
around Mt Zion in Jerusalem but the broad definition is the establishing =
of an=20
idealized civilization for all who want it. The Tribe/Nation of Judah =
became the=20
world's largest adoption agency. </FONT></DIV>
<DIV><FONT size=3D2 face=3DArial></FONT> </DIV>
<DIV><FONT size=3D2 face=3DArial>Any person of sound mind will seek an =
idealized way=20
of life, a way of life which is good, better and best. Epstein wrote in =
the=20
scholarly journal "Judaism" circa 1980 that Judaism, contrary to popular =
belief=20
is a proselytizing religion. He summarizes ten major

historical waves of =

proselytizing. Christianity itself is the result of teaching and =
preaching=20
Judaism by TJWSHWG who said not one jot or tittle of the Hebrew law was =
changed=20
by Him.When both the spirit of the law and the application of the law =
are=20
balanced out, this becomes possible. </FONT><FONT size=3D2 =
face=3DArial>For example=20
a letter of the law prohibition against eating shellfish is sound when =
the=20
properties of these creatures are not well known and some are poisonous. =
The=20
spirit of the law has to do with good health and other principles. =
Health=20
knowledge changes the application of the law but the law itself does not =
change.=20
The traditional principles for civilization dating back thousands of =
years=20
applies today and that Israelite way of life exists today for all who =
want=20
it.</FONT></DIV>
<DIV><FONT size=3D2 face=3DArial></FONT> </DIV>
<DIV><FONT size=3D2 face=3DArial>Who then are the neo-Israelites? Is the =
Golden Calf=20
Cult is now accepted without censure in modern day Israel? Modern Israel =
is a=20
nation which does not even know the language spoken by the original =
Israelite=20
(Jacob) and his sons in Egypt. They also did not have the Ten =
Commandments until=20
they left Egypt. How then can Israelite civilization be

established, =
based on=20
tradition? That can only happen if the PRINCIPLES are
adhered to (like =
those of=20
the Decalogue) while the PRACTICES are adapted to time
and place. =
Otherwise, do=20
young Canadians today repudiate the Bible and God's Law
when they =
venture into=20
mining colonies on the Moon later in this century? What
is their =
description of=20
even one neo-Israelite civilization for BC and export
when there could =
be=20
many?</FONT></DIV>
<DIV><FONT size=3D2 face=3DArial></FONT> </DIV>
<DIV><FONT size=3D2 face=3DArial>GOODNESS is a
principle. It was chosen =
by Solomon=20
when he was told to make a choice by God. It is a
repeated again and =
again in=20
Red Letter and black letter writings of the Bible. That
summarizing =
principle=20
applies to all of the particular practices of
civilization. We respect =
our=20
religious ancestors from the ancient world but they
lived under =
primitive=20
conditions with limited knowledge. Primitives world-
wide understood =
blood=20
sacrifice as an offering which they imagined would
please those in the=20
hereafter. Just as the Sabbath was made for man, not
man for the =
Sabbath, blood=20
sacrifices were made for man and not vice-versa. In Red
Letters we read =
"Though=20
ye offer me burnt offerings and your meat offerings, I
will not accept =

them"=20
(Amos 5:22). Psalm 40, verse 6 tells us "Sacrifice and offering thou =
didst not=20
desire". </FONT><FONT size=3D2 face=3DArial>Likewise God asks in Psalm =
50:13, =20
"Will I eat the flesh of bulls, or drink the blood of goats?" The theme =
is 100%=20
consistent that the way of life demanded by the Almighty is that which =
is IHS=20
(In His Service).</FONT></DIV>
<DIV><FONT size=3D2 face=3DArial></FONT> </DIV>
<DIV><FONT size=3D2 face=3DArial>ASK THE EXPERTS!</FONT></DIV>
<DIV><FONT size=3D2 face=3DArial></FONT> </DIV>
<DIV><FONT size=3D2 face=3DArial><STRONG><U>CHAPTER 8: </U>NOW IS THE =
TIME,=20
CANADA</STRONG></FONT></DIV>
<DIV><FONT size=3D2 face=3DArial></FONT> </DIV>
<DIV><FONT face=3DArial></FONT> </DIV>
<DIV><FONT size=3D2 face=3DArial><FONT color=3D#ff0000 =
size=3D3><STRONG>Behold, I have=20
put my words in your mouth</STRONG></FONT> - Jeremiah 1:9</FONT></DIV>
<DIV><FONT size=3D2 face=3DArial></FONT> </DIV>
<DIV><FONT size=3D2 face=3DArial>"Now is the time for all good men to =
come to the=20
aid of the Party". That used to be the first exercise of multi-digit =
typing=20
students just as "Hello world!" is the first C programming exercise at =
BCIT.=20
What if there are no good men to come to the aid of the "Party of God" =
and=20
program GODBOT? What if there are no good, honest people to give good, =
honest=20
answers to good, honest questions? What if Catholic and Protestantism =

catechisms=20
are disingenuous and all these so-called experts who write them can do =
when=20
asked about a Christian civilization here for export off-planet is evade =
the=20
questions and issues? In the words of Canadian balladeer Leonard Cohen =
(CD-The=20
Future):</FONT></DIV>
<DIV><FONT size=3D2 face=3DArial></FONT> </DIV>
<DIV><FONT size=3D2 face=3DArial>Everybody knows the dice were =
loaded,</FONT></DIV>
<DIV><FONT size=3D2 face=3DArial>Everybody knows the game was =
rigged,</FONT></DIV>
<DIV><FONT size=3D2 face=3DArial>Everybody knows the good guys =
lost.</FONT></DIV>
<DIV><FONT size=3D2 face=3DArial>Everybody knows.</FONT></DIV>
<DIV><FONT size=3D2 face=3DArial></FONT> </DIV>
<DIV><FONT size=3D2 face=3DArial>We cannot have peace, order and good =
government=20
unless there are those in leadership positions (parliamentary and =
religious=20
institutions) who want to end the bad features of civilization in and =
around us=20
advance the good features. Again, that sounds childlike yet it was the =
request=20
of King Solomon. There is child-like simplicity in such a statement but =
the=20
testing of it goes wanting. Are the lyrics of "The Future" telling us =
something=20
about human nature which political slogans avoid and religion experts =
flee from?=20
In CCC or Catechism of the Catholic Church (p 801) the reader is told to =

"test=20
all things" citing I Thess. 5:12 which is similarly stated as "prove all =
things"=20
in the KJV Bible (hereafter "p" refers to paragraph rather than =
page).Upon=20
questioning almost all people will say "I am doing my best" when asked =
about=20
work performance or role in life like parental role. The GODBOT test is =
to start=20
anew. That is not utopian where utopian connotes unrealistic or pie in =
the sky.=20
Wilderness preceded all cities today and the space age preparations of =
this new=20
generation force the planning of such cities/civilizations. A city on =
the Moon=20
or Mars does not "just happen". Therein we have a proper test for the=20
political-religious catechism experts who claim to be doing their best =
today for=20
the current ongoing civilization. Will they come forward from Ottawa to =
plan a=20
"CANOPOLIS" in BC and compete against other models of civilization? If =
they flee=20
from this p 801 test, they are no experts in the catechism of a way of =
life. CCC=20
gives an excellent rule for all such experts regardless of their =
background,=20
politics or religion. </FONT><FONT size=3D2 face=3DArial>If the words of =
the experts=20
truly come from God, will they say He has put His words in their mouths? =
Former=20
BC Premier WAC Bennett liked to say, "I am plugged in to =

God".</FONT></DIV>
<DIV><FONT size=3D2 face=3DArial></FONT> </DIV>
<DIV><FONT size=3D2 face=3DArial>At the time of this writing, =
billionaire and=20
presidential candidate Donald =E2=80=9Cbest of the best=E2=80=9D Trump =
is planning a new office=20
tower for Vancouver. If he were to build it as first structure of a BC =
CANOPOLIS=20
and a replica of Building 7 from the 9/11 horror, that would provide an =
amazing=20
test and a tribute to American culture, exported to Canada, Building 7 =
according=20
to the official report tumbled into its own basement at almost free-fall =
speed.=20
Over 90% of it was pulverized so the mass of twisted steel did not occur =
as=20
expected. The word =E2=80=9Cmiraculous=E2=80=9D is not too strong. This =
was reportedly caused by=20
=E2=80=9Cmiracle oil=E2=80=9D (jet fuel) spilled onto one corner near =
the top. Trump Tower could=20
have a Building 7 surrogate tested before the heavy (red iron) structure =
is=20
filled in with offices. If it can be razed this way, the demolition =
industry is=20
greatly advanced. When it comes time to raze the Trump Tower perhaps a =
century=20
from now, all that has to be done is to pour some miracle oil on it. =
What a cost=20
saving! </FONT></DIV>
<DIV><FONT size=3D2 face=3DArial></FONT> </DIV>
<DIV><FONT size=3D2 face=3DArial>The UN is a debating club for criminals =
and despots=20
of the world. The ICC might as well be dubbed the

International Court of =

Criminals. UN does not even represent the people of its
200 or so nation =
members=20
and ignores THOUSANDS of potential nation members like
First Nations =
across=20
Canada, Basques, Kurds, Welsh, Scots and many others.
</FONT><FONT =
size=3D2=20
face=3DArial>After they are liberated from Ottawa's
colonialist resource =
theft, BC=20
First Nations may invite any of these foreign nations
to provide =
cultural=20
expression on long term leases as Hong Kong once had.
BC Indians are =
mindful of=20
the painful history in which their nationhood was only
mockingly given =
credence=20
by Ottawa. </FONT></DIV>
<DIV><FONT size=3D2 face=3DArial></FONT> </DIV>
<DIV><FONT size=3D2 face=3DArial>ASK THE
EXPERTS!</FONT></DIV>
<DIV><FONT size=3D2 face=3DArial></FONT> </DIV>
<DIV><FONT size=3D2 face=3DArial></FONT> </DIV>
<DIV><FONT size=3D2 face=3DArial><STRONG><U>CHAPTER 9:
</U>QUESTIONS =
ABOUT THE=20
CANADIAN GOLD WAR</STRONG></FONT></DIV>
<DIV><FONT size=3D2 face=3DArial></FONT> </DIV>
<DIV><FONT size=3D2 face=3DArial></FONT> </DIV>
<DIV><FONT size=3D2 face=3DArial><FONT color=3D#ff0000
=
size=3D3><STRONG>Thy silver and=20
thy gold is mine</STRONG></FONT> - I Kings
20:3</FONT></DIV>
<DIV><FONT size=3D2 face=3DArial></FONT> </DIV>
<DIV><FONT size=3D2 face=3DArial>Gold War by Rock
Hunter was given the =
ISBN=20
978-0-9937593-1-4 by the Library of Parliament system.
It was then =
published by=20

Xulon Press.</FONT></DIV>
<DIV><FONT size=3D2 face=3DArial></FONT> </DIV>
<DIV><FONT size=3D2 face=3DArial>Gold War tells the
story of how Frank =
Paul, a=20
homeless Micmac Indian, was killed in Vancouver by what
was in effect an =

extra-judicial execution. He was taken from a confining
and yet warm and =

health-sustainiing jail cell by VPD and placed in his
"home" in an alley =
where=20
(like others before and since) he died of exposure and
=
homelessness-related=20
adversity. This fatal result was predictable on a
probability basis and =
it is=20
predictable every day in Canada when people are forced
into conditions =
of indoor=20
and outdoor homelessness. You might call it a Russian-
roulette form of =
Canadian=20
"justice". If Frank had come before the McLaughlin
Supreme Court in 2001 =
instead=20
of Louise Gosselin one would expect the same result
unless the justice =
system=20
were to practice a very strange form of affirmative
action. The result =
would be=20
a macabre measure to establish extra-judicial capital
punishment ratios =
related=20
to race and gender and ethnicity. Should the judicial
system be allowed =
to kill=20
a French Canadian woman (Gosselin) with the same
alacrity as killing an =
Indian=20
Canadian man (Paul)?</FONT></DIV>
<DIV><FONT size=3D2 face=3DArial></FONT> </DIV>
<DIV><FONT size=3D2 face=3DArial>Demographic parameters

are entangled in =
the=20
thousands of cases of homelessness whereby health
damaging and life =
destroying=20
conditions are actively forced or passively allowed.
Both active and =
passive=20
factors are under the control of governing
administrations. Does it =
exonerate=20
these authorities if the demographics are disentangled?
The McLaughlin =
et al=20
opinion of 2001 would not deem it unlawful or unjust
for a Louise =
Gosselin to be=20
placed in health and life destroying conditions so why
would it not =
declare the=20
Frank Paul death to be lawful and just? If one
demographic in particular =
is=20
disentangled (First Nation) is that no longer a clear
matter of =
genocide? The=20
conscience of Constable Instant says
otherwise.</FONT></DIV>
<DIV><FONT size=3D2 face=3DArial></FONT> </DIV>
<DIV><FONT size=3D2 face=3DArial>Note that there is a
SYSTEM of that =
which is=20
bad/evil which is being decried. Does the political-
judicial system of =
Canada=20
serves good or bad? What does it make of Solomon's
choice? Otherwise =
___________=20
is a good feature because ___________________.
Individuals like a tearful=20
Constable Instant of VPD are not blamed for the death
of Frank Paul. =
They are=20
only following orders in the genocide of the Indian
people and poor =
people of=20
Canada. According to the SCC majority of 2001 it is

"justified' to force =
a Frank=20
Paul into conditions of indoor and outdoor homelessness
which are KNOWN =
in=20
advance to have a Russian-roulette probability of
causing death because =
nobody=20
has a duty to sustain his life they say. They added
that it would be too =
costly=20
to sustain the lives of such people which is not
credible when we have =
the fact=20
that a generation earlier homelessness in Canada was a
rarity so the=20
administrative system WAS sustaining the lives of
people with the =
"wrong"=20
demographic features (like poor, Indian, alcoholic,
mentally ill). =
Justice was=20
cheapened in 2001 and cheapened to a shameful and
shocking degree =
mindful of=20
what Hitler called his "useless eaters" policy.
Although Canada is by=20
Charter/Constitution a "democratic society" perhaps
even more democratic =

measures like the recall of Supreme Court judges
for malpractice =
should be=20
instituted. If it is argued that Frank Paul himself
chose the alley, one =
must=20
examine more closely the torturous conditions of indoor
facilities =
called=20
=E2=80=9Cshelters=E2=80=9D which are in fact torture
chambers. Consider =
Vancouver=E2=80=99s =E2=80=9CAnchor of=20
Hope=E2=80=9D on Cordova Street where 100 people sleep
on mats a few =
inches from each=20
other. Airborne diseases like TB and influenza are
spread rapidly. Half =

of the=20
cases of TB in all of British Columbia are within a few
blocks of this =
=E2=80=9CAnchor=20
of Hell=E2=80=9D. What kind of choice did Frank Paul
have?</FONT></DIV>
<DIV><FONT size=3D2 face=3DArial></FONT> </DIV>
<DIV><FONT size=3D2 face=3DArial>Given that cost is an
issue though the =
tragic death=20
of Frank Paul and the death and degradation of others
by homelessness is =
given a=20
remedy in Gold War. BC will soon be proven as the new
South Africa of =
precious=20
metal mining with trillions of dollars in new mineral
wealth. The dozen =
or so=20
major Indian national groupings here will start the
process of =
uncoupling from=20
Canada. Paid for in minerals, a contest of
civilizations will result. =
What we=20
witnessed in 2001 was anathema to civilization.
CANOPOLIS contestants =
can=20
suggest ways to solve this social problem and many
others.</FONT></DIV>
<DIV><FONT size=3D2 face=3DArial></FONT> </DIV>
<DIV><FONT size=3D2 face=3DArial>ASK THE
EXPERTS!</FONT></DIV>
<DIV><FONT size=3D2 face=3DArial></FONT> </DIV>
<DIV><FONT size=3D2 face=3DArial><STRONG><U>CHAPTER 10:
</U>CATHOLIC =
CANADIAN=20
CIVILIZATION</STRONG></FONT></DIV>
<DIV><FONT face=3DArial></FONT> </DIV>
<DIV><FONT color=3D#ff0000 face=3DArial><STRONG>I have
set before you =
life and=20
death, blessing and cursing. Choose life
</STRONG><FONT =
color=3D#000000=20
size=3D2><STRONG>-</STRONG> Deuteronomy
30:19</FONT></FONT></DIV>

<DIV><STRONG><FONT size=3D2
face=3DArial></FONT></STRONG> </DIV>
<DIV><FONT size=3D2 face=3DArial>Why would Catholic
civilization as a =
"culture of=20
life" not be EAGER to lead such a competition of
civilizations in BC? =
The pages=20
of Catholic Catechism (CC) abound in authoritative
statements about the=20
superiority of Catholic social-political-economic
theory and practice. =
Further=20
to the CC p 801 "test all things" directive the
teaching masters behind =
those=20
2,865 paragraphs should be glad of the opportunity to
do so. Many =
thousands of=20
particular services are found under Canadian
constitutional "supremacy =
of God=20
and the rule of law". What if Parliament were to export
a Catholic =
CANOPOLIS to=20
liberated British Columbia with its particular spin on
all of those=20
political-legal services? It would claim IHS (In His
Service) supremacy =
over all=20
animal sacrifices as explained in Chapter 7. The
sacrifice demanded =
however is=20
to sacrifice that which is bad and embrace that which
is good as I =
Thess. 5:21=20
says to "hold fast that which is good".</FONT></DIV>
<DIV><FONT size=3D2 face=3DArial></FONT> </DIV>
<DIV><FONT size=3D2 face=3DArial>The opening statements
of CC invite the =
entire=20
world to the table of CC questions and answers.
Catholic religion =
includes over=20
one billion adherents and one million clergy (priests,
monks, deacons, =
nuns et=20

al). It includes millions of experts in secular
sciences, arts, law etc. =
How=20
well can it compete with over one billion Muslims
before the "Parliament =
of=20
Man"? Surely Muslims, Hindus, Buddhists and many other
religions would =
also=20
claim adherence to "hold fast that which is good" as a
slogan. Can they =
stand up=20
to the testing/proof which takes place when good,
honest questions are =
put=20
forward?</FONT></DIV>
<DIV><FONT size=3D2 face=3DArial></FONT> </DIV>
<DIV><FONT size=3D2 face=3DArial>One has to wonder
about the =
relationship between=20
Catholic and American world outlooks in historical
context. Diplomatic=20
relationships between the Papal States/Holy See/Vatican
were stopped =
between=20
1867 and 1984. That is a long time and it was a most
serious policy =
decision. It=20
was caused by facts and suspicions over the Lincoln
assassination. =
Conspirators=20
met at the boarding house of Mary Surratt of Catholic
religion and she =
was=20
executed for her part in the plot. The suspicions had
to do with how far =
up the=20
hierarchy this went. Charles Morse of Morse code fame
and the Canadian =
Catholic=20
priest Chiniquy reported controversial material on what
they knew of the =
plot.=20
Chiniquy may have also been the most widely read
Canadian author of his =
day. All=20
these names and events can be researched by Internet.

But this is the =
era of=20
space colonization and American plans for space
colonization compete =
with=20
Catholic plans. The Rock Hunter letter of October 9,
2014 adds an up to =
date=20
note to these historical issues and it is photocopied
here. It speaks =
for=20
itself. Chiniquy never revoked small-c catholicism,
defined as =
universalism. He=20
might ask today for an articulation of this Canadian =
universality.</FONT></DIV>
<DIV><FONT size=3D2 face=3DArial></FONT> </DIV>
<DIV><FONT size=3D2 face=3DArial>Articulation comes in
the form of a =
CANOPOLIS which=20
can migrate off-planet without limit in time-space. It
is tempting to =
think of=20
the Sto:lo legendary sky-born people as post-flood,
post-Noah humans =
from space=20
but that idea might upset Notre Dame University and
Salve Regina as =
=E2=80=9CNew Age=E2=80=9D.=20
Yet absence of evidence is not evidence of absence. The
Bible says =
nothing about=20
pyramids or saber-toothed tigers or giant cave bears.
The Bible does not =

describe the =E2=80=9Cgiants=E2=80=9D on the Earth
cited in Genesis. =
Were they animals (like the=20
mammoths which co-habited with man), were they humans
or were these =
people=20
mental and psychological giants as the Sto:lo sky-born
people are said =
to be?=20
From early Barbra Streisand music:</FONT></DIV>
<DIV><FONT size=3D2 face=3DArial></FONT> </DIV>
<DIV><FONT color=3D#0000ff size=3D2

```
face=3DArial><STRONG>As I was =
travelling across=20
the sky, this lovely planet caught my
eye,</STRONG></FONT></DIV>
<DIV><FONT color=3D#0000ff size=3D2
face=3DArial><STRONG>Being curious I =
flew close=20
by, and now we=E2=80=99re caught here til we
die.</STRONG></FONT></DIV>
<DIV><FONT size=3D2 face=3DArial></FONT> </DIV>
<DIV><FONT size=3D2 face=3DArial>The closing
couplet:</FONT></DIV>
<DIV><FONT size=3D2 face=3DArial></FONT> </DIV>
<DIV><FONT color=3D#0000ff size=3D2
face=3DArial><STRONG>Some day =
we=E2=80=9911 all change=20
into peaceful men,</STRONG></FONT></DIV>
<DIV><FONT color=3D#0000ff size=3D2
face=3DArial><STRONG>And =
we=E2=80=9911 return into the=20
sky</STRONG></FONT></DIV>
<DIV><FONT size=3D2 face=3DArial></FONT> </DIV>
<DIV><FONT size=3D2 face=3DArial>ASK THE
EXPERTS!</FONT></DIV>
<DIV><FONT size=3D2 face=3DArial></FONT> </DIV>
<DIV><FONT size=3D2 face=3DArial><STRONG><U>CHAPTER 11:
</U>JUDAIC =
CANADIAN=20
TESTS</STRONG></FONT></DIV>
<DIV><STRONG><U><FONT size=3D2 =
face=3DArial></FONT></U></STRONG> </DIV>
<DIV><FONT size=3D2 face=3DArial><STRONG><FONT
color=3D#ff0000 =
size=3D3>Heaven and earth=20
shall pass away, but my words shall not pass
away</FONT></STRONG>  =
-=20
Matthew 24:35</FONT></DIV>
<DIV><FONT size=3D2 face=3DArial></FONT> </DIV>
<DIV><FONT size=3D2 face=3DArial>This assertion by
TJWSHWG is =
effectively a=20
repetition of Isaiah 51:6. God says the heavens shall
pass away like =
smoke which=20
is in itself an amazing revelation considering that
human cosmological =
```

science=20
has only recently generated models of how the universe
will pass away. =
God also=20
says in Isaiah that His words shall not pass
away.</FONT></DIV>
<DIV><FONT size=3D2 face=3DArial></FONT> </DIV>
<DIV><FONT size=3D2 face=3DArial>"Judaism has never
called for an =
unreasoning faith"=20
we read in the De Sola Pool Traditional Jewish Prayer
Book. Jews "test =
all=20
things'" (properly) by sacred tradition. There is no
sacred scripture to =
an=20
unknowing mineral species. The light shines in the
darkness of the rocks =
and the=20
darkness comprehends it not. The light of the Judahite
faith is given as =
a=20
blessing for comprehending persons. "Salvation is of
the Jews" Jesus =
said.=20
Sacred writings or words from antiquity cannot be
comprehended without =
the light=20
of truth which comes from the Almighty. "in Judaism,
the flesh became =
words.=20
Words were the traditional refuge of the Jewish people"
(page 54 of "The =
Talmud=20
and the Internet by Rosen). Rosen also describes a
traditional Jewish =
custom=20
whereby Scriptural messages are written in cake/bread
which is then =
eaten. This=20
hearkens to Ezekial 3:2 and also to John 6:41. The
literal and =
metaphorical=20
relationship of those passages to the Eucharist or Last
Supper ritual is =
of=20
course left to the experts. But undeniably, TJWSHWG

declared that unless =
we=20
abide in Him there is no life in us and that the
resurrection of the =
body for=20
the Israelite faithful as described in Ezekial is by
Him.</FONT></DIV>
<DIV><FONT size=3D2 face=3DArial></FONT> </DIV>
<DIV><FONT size=3D2 face=3DArial>Scripture trumps
tradition and teaching =
so the=20
metaphor of three pillars requires some elaboration.
The second two =
pillars=20
stand upon the first. They are not equal. The
particular form of =
tradition=20
changes even while meaning may remain constant to the
practitioners. No=20
tradition or teaching can be upheld by the faithful if
it is in =
opposition to=20
Scripture and to repeat the passage above, Scripture
can only be =
compehended,=20
sola gracia. </FONT><FONT size=3D2 face=3DArial>In the
Red Letters of =
TJWSHWG, an=20
Israelite of the Tribe of Judah, we read, "Heaven and
earth shall pass =
away but=20
my words shall not pass away" (Matthew 24:35). God's
MEANING in His =
words about=20
Israel shall never pass away. "As the lily dies only
when iits scent =
fouls, so=20
Israel will not die so long as it executes the commands
of the Torah and =
does=20
good deeds" (De Sola Pool, page 879). De Sola Pool adds,
"The word Torah =
means=20
teaching" and Rosen says "The Torah is celebrated as
the living word of =
God"=20
(page 65). What do poiltical-religious experts say

about the daily way =
of life=20
for those people who can imagine living in a
civilization which is "the =
best of=20
the best"? If 600,000 nomadic people could gather at a
mountain several =
thousand=20
years ago and found a new and enlightened nation IHS,
why not 100,000 =
today in=20
British Columbia en route to an off-planet colony with
a plan taught to =
them for=20
the living word of TJWSHWG?</FONT><FONT size=3D2
face=3DArial>. =
</FONT></DIV>
<DIV><FONT size=3D2 face=3DArial></FONT> </DIV>
<DIV><FONT size=3D2 face=3DArial>Given the paper of
Epstein as cited =
above on=20
proselytizing Judaism, we could say that Zionism is for
everyone. =
Zionism as the=20
establishing of an ideal civilization in this world is
found in every =
book of=20
the Bible. It is found in every political-religious
book. "Ziophobic" =
people=20
avoid this clear and positive meaning of Zionism. A
reasoned approach to =

physical and metaphysical phenomena is required by the
history of sacred =

traditions of the Judahite people. Reasoning with God
is invited in Red =
Letters=20
by the book of Isaiah as even having the power to cure
sin. Where would =
we be=20
today if the Jews and Romans of 2,000 years ago in
Judea had decided to =
reason=20
with words instead of torture and murder? Who are the
teaching masters, =

the=20
magisterium, of Judahite faith? Who has exposed the science fraud of =
Cohen Y=20
chromosome propaganda to use a specific example of reasoning at work? =
Shlomo=20
Sand writes in "When And How The Jewish People Was Invented" in accord =
with=20
Epstein that "varied peoples converted to Judaism during the course of =
history"=20
and that modern Jews "are not at all the descendents of ancient people =
who=20
inhabiited the Kingdom of Juda during the First and Second Temple =
Period". This=20
book, published in Haaretz by Ofri Ilani calls Jewish geneology tracings =
today a=20
"national mythology". That mythology must include the Cohen Y =
chromosome.=20
Because of the phonetic similarity of the name Cohen to that of the =
Cohanim=20
priesthood in Ancient Israel, a scientific thesis was put forward that =
Cohen Y=20
chromosome constancy dated back to that era and that region. But dating =
a=20
chromosome back 3,000 years is questionable at best (because of the =
unknown=20
variation in mutation rate over those centuries) and even if validated =
it proves=20
nothing. Chromosomes do not have surnames in double helix chemistry. The =

original family name bearing this chromosome is not known. Dogmatic =
declarations=20
about region of origin are even more speculative.

"Middle East" is a =
huge region=20
which goes even beyond Greater Israel (Nile to
Euphrates). Ancient =
people were=20
also well travelled as the silk roads (plural) through
Afghanistan and =
Pakistan=20
prove. Do a search on Karakoram Highway, the 8th wonder
of the world. =
The Cohen=20
Y chromosome even claims a historical occurrence in the
Lamba tribe of =
southern=20
Africa. It is generally accepted that the surname Cohen
and all =
variations like=20
Kahan, Cohn, Cohen, Kaplan and about 50 others are
derived from the name =

Kaganovitch/Kagan which originated between the Black
and Caspian seas. =
In accord=20
with Shlomo Sand's position that many Jews today are
"for the most part=20
descendents of pagans who converted to Judaism" the
pagan name =
Kaganovitch seems=20
more likely to have a Japhethite history rather than
Shemite/Semite and =
it was=20
"modernized" to Kahan which is the phonetic root of all
the later =
variants.=20
Constancy of the chromosome is easily achieved by the
expulsion or =
elimination=20
of illegitimate male children and by having no male
adoptions. Kagans =
and others=20
converted to Judaism during one of the waves of
proselytizing as =
discussed by=20
Epstein., in this case the 7th to 11th centuries
AD. Consider =
again the=20
role of silk roads as names wander far and wide with

their owners. We =
read on=20
the wiki/Khan_(title) that Kagan is also a title which
means "sovereign =
or=20
military ruler" and that Ghenghis Khan is a famous
example of this =
title. "His=20
title was Khagan ('Khan of Khans', see below, but is
oftened shortened =
to Khan".=20
</FONT></DIV>
<DIV><FONT size=3D2 face=3DArial></FONT> </DIV>
<DIV><FONT size=3D2 face=3DArial>Some, like Professor
Shlomo Sand may =
argue that=20
Jewish civilization is "invented" or created but that
is not derogatory =
in any=20
way. On the contrary it is a stroke of genius which
recognizes facts in =
the=20
historical record. There is almost no record, Biblical
or secular, which =

describes what the Israelites did over 400 years in
Egypt before the =
Exodus=20
circa 1450 BC. Hebrew language can only be traced back
to circa 1,000 BC =
so we=20
do not even have a record of the language spoken by
Jacob/Israel or =
Moses.=20
Creativity is not a fault or vice. How could the
Israelites not be =
culturally=20
creative as Jacob's small family grew to a nation of
600,000 =
subordinated to=20
Egyptian cultural masters, under the Babylonian
captivity and then Roman =

occupation? Each would lead to intermarriage with
adversarial cultures =
and thus=20
biological as well as cultural transformation. We read

in "The Standard =
Jewish=20
Encyclopedia" (1966, page 594) that "The Edomites were
conquered by John =

Hyrcanus who forcibly converted them to Judaism and
from then on they=20
constituted part of the Jewish people, Herod being one
of their =
descendents".=20
The Israellites were people of law but all nations who
have ever =
inhabited Earth=20
are populated by people of law. No society has ever
existed here in a =
state of=20
chaos which is what some seem to be advocating when
they talk about "The =

Singularity" of transhumanism as an imminent social-
political event. =
That is=20
folly. The question then is what law code applicable to
the time and =
place of=20
this space era might a Neo-Judaic civilization generate
or invent. Not =
one jot=20
or tittle of The Law changes but the spirit of the law
is adaptive. =
Good,=20
healthful dieting never changes as a principle of law.
The particulars =
of diet=20
and dining etiquette do change. Some traditions are
deemed sacred and =
are=20
resistant to change but they do change in practice
while staying =
constant in=20
principle. </FONT></DIV>
<DIV><FONT size=3D2 face=3DArial></FONT> </DIV>
<DIV><FONT size=3D2 face=3DArial>What blessings will
British Columbian =
cultural=20
inventions bring the world? The Cold War was won by the
test of gates. =

Open the=20
gates or borders between nations and see which way the
population moves. =
Who=20
will move into the liberated nations of a free and
balkanized British =
Columbia?=20
What designs for future civilization and future sapiens
will originate =
with the=20
present day nations whose colonialist ancestors came
here in the 1700s =
and=20
1800s? Gold War explains how Russia, United States,
Great Britain, Spain =
and=20
Canada were major rivals. Canada won the colonialism
contest for BC with =
the=20
illegal colonialist annexation of this region in 1871.
But this was not =
a just=20
or legal victory. Canada has no claim over the natural
resources of BC =
from=20
justice, military conquest or any other rationale. What
do the political =
parties=20
of Canada as represented in Parliament say to this in
Question Period? =
What do=20
the Conservative, Liberal, Green and New Democratic
parties say? What =
does the=20
Bloc Quebecois party say? What does BQ say to a Bloc
Indian Party (BIP) =
in BC?=20
Such a party could easily be registered by UBCIC (Union
of BC Indian =
Chiefs) and=20
the sea to sea to sea AFN (Assembly of First Nations).
It can be =
discussed as a=20
matter of national importance without runniing in a
single election. =
Does BQ=20
accept its platform of UN membership for BC First

Nations? Does BQ =
accept a=20
generalization of that UN membership to the northern
Cree or southern =
Iroquois=20
of Quebec?</FONT></DIV>
<DIV><FONT size=3D2 face=3DArial></FONT> </DIV>
<DIV><FONT size=3D2 face=3DArial>Modern
=E2=80=9CIsrael=E2=80=9D appears =
to be a conglomerate of=20
revived Edomite, Midian, Hittite, Canaanite and other
micro-nations from =
the=20
past of the Arabian Peninsula region
(=E2=80=9CLevant=E2=80=9D). How =
else can one explain Golda=20
Meier=E2=80=99s lament about the 1/3 Atheists in her
flock? Moses would =
have immediately=20
killed such people amongst his flock.</FONT></DIV>
<DIV><FONT size=3D2 face=3DArial>The resurrection
referred to in Ezekial =
and Daniel=20
which appears to have impacted Greco-Roman metaphysical
philosophy can =
be=20
collectively and metaphorically applied to a
resurrected Israellite =
CANOPOLIS of=20
100,000. Or should that be 100,000 x 12 with a
CANOPOLIS for each tribe? =
Since=20
we know so little about the ancient civilizations of
Jacob (Israel) and =
his twin=20
brother, Esau (Edom) how can we today match latter-day
Israel with =
latter-day=20
Edom? What kind of civilization would law and justice
scholars describe =
today=20
for each according to the ideals of each twin? Apply
that also to the =
chapter=20
below on Chinese Canadian Civilization.</FONT></DIV>
<DIV><FONT size=3D2 face=3DArial>Historically there are
precedents for =

electing=20
kings. Both New Israel and New Edom might elect their
=E2=80=9CKing of =
the Jews=E2=80=9D as a=20
modern Herod.</FONT></DIV>
<DIV><FONT size=3D2 face=3DArial></FONT> </DIV>
<DIV><FONT size=3D2 face=3DArial>Again, from Leonard
Cohen and The=20
Future:</FONT></DIV>
<DIV><FONT size=3D2 face=3DArial></FONT> </DIV>
<DIV><FONT color=3D#0000ff size=3D2
face=3DArial><STRONG>It=E2=80=99s =
once for the Devil and=20
it=E2=80=99s once for Christ,</STRONG></FONT></DIV>
<DIV><FONT color=3D#0000ff size=3D2
face=3DArial><STRONG>But the Boss =
don=E2=80=99t like these=20
dizzy heights,</STRONG></FONT></DIV>
<DIV><FONT color=3D#0000ff size=3D2
face=3DArial><STRONG>We=E2=80=99re =
busted in the blinding=20
lights,</STRONG></FONT></DIV>
<DIV><FONT color=3D#0000ff size=3D2
face=3DArial><STRONG>Of closing=20
time</STRONG>.</FONT></DIV>
<DIV><FONT face=3DCalibri></FONT> </DIV>
<DIV><FONT size=3D2 face=3DArial>ASK THE
EXPERTS!</FONT></DIV>
<DIV><FONT size=3D2 face=3DArial></FONT> </DIV>
<DIV><FONT size=3D2 face=3DArial></FONT> </DIV>
<DIV><FONT size=3D2 face=3DArial><STRONG><U>CHAPTER
12</U>: MUSLIM =
CANADIAN=20
CIVILIZATION</STRONG></FONT></DIV>
<DIV><FONT size=3D2 face=3DArial></FONT> </DIV>
<DIV><FONT size=3D2 face=3DArial></FONT> </DIV>
<DIV><FONT face=3DArial><FONT size=3D2><STRONG><FONT
color=3D#ff0000 =
size=3D3>And the=20
land which I gave to Abraham and Isaac, I will give to
you and your=20
seed</FONT></STRONG> - Genesis 35:12</FONT></FONT></DIV>
<DIV><FONT size=3D2 face=3DArial></FONT> </DIV>
<DIV><FONT size=3D2 face=3DArial>Rushdie found himself
under a fatwa =
(religion-based=20
death threat) for publishing his book about Koran under

the title =
Satanic=20
Verses. But we use an expression like THE Koran without
thinking what a =
small=20
and important word means - <U><STRONG>THE</STRONG></U>.
Any Koran is =
only a set=20
of markings on paper or other medium unless it is
interpreted There may =
be as=20
many interpretations as there are readers. Whose is
correct? Whose is =
satanic?=20
If a code of law is generated from
<STRONG><U>A</U></STRONG> Koran, =
whose code=20
is to be accepted as the foundation for a Muslim
civilization in BC? =
Koran=20
originated with an Arab commander-in-chief, Mohammed
Abdullah whose =
empire is=20
the most successful the world has ever seen without
leaving home, the=20
Mecca-Medina region. His words on religion pertain to
truncated =
references on=20
about only 25 Biblical personages out of the hundreds
in a Bible. They =
are also=20
sayings which were independently understood by many
others with the name =
of=20
Mohammed which was common even then. These ideas like
the repudiation of =
the=20
Holy Trinity were circulated by millions of people in
the Middle East =
and=20
Mediterranean region. It took 25 years or so after the
death of Mohammed =

Abdulladh for Caliph Bakr to gather the beliefs into a
single book, =
called=20
Koran. That was written in Classical Arabic so the

problem of multiple=20
interpretations is complicated further. Few people
today understand =
Classical=20
Arabic.</FONT></DIV>
<DIV><FONT size=3D2 face=3DArial></FONT> </DIV>
<DIV><FONT size=3D2 face=3DArial>Muslim foundations in
Koran and =
associated law=20
(sometimes called Sharia) do however have some
constancies like =
rejection of=20
Trinitarian teaching and another important one is the
rejection of the =
Red=20
Letter words of the Bible on inheritance law pertaining
to the =
descendents of=20
Abraham. In Genesis 15:18 we find these Red
Letter words =
identifying a=20
super-nation between the Nile and Euphrates rivers. In
Genesis18:18 God =
says all=20
the persons of the earth shall be blessed in Abraham
and his =
super-nation but in=20
Genesis 35:12 God says with perfect clarity that the
land which was =
given to=20
Abraham and then his son Isaac is passed on further to
Israel, son of =
Isaac and=20
in Israel all the people of the earth shall be blessed
(Genesis 28:14). =
That=20
also seems to explain the Koranic truncation of
Biblical messages as =
cited=20
above. Muslim civilization cannot accept the Biblical
God whose central=20
inheritance in the Middle East names Israel as having
rightful title to =
all that=20
is called Saudi Arabia today, including Mecca and
Medina. That =
Mecca-Medina=20

region is immediately southward of modern Jordan which is Biblical Edom. =
It was=20
called Midian and Moses was quite familiar with it as the territory of =
his=20
distant cousins. Ottawa politicians may prefer to avoid the contentious =
issues=20
of religion but they cannot be avoided if anyone is to understand the =
war raging=20
from North Africa to Afghanistan today and its result at home in a =
Vancouver Sun=20
headline like that of October 23, 2014, "Terror Rocks The Nation's =
Capital".=20
History and ideology (beliefs) underlie such events.</FONT></DIV>
<DIV><FONT size=3D2 face=3DArial></FONT> </DIV>
<DIV><FONT size=3D2 face=3DArial>Multiculturalism as a political =
platform however,=20
can still take a positive stance. The same test applies to all cultures =
in=20
Canada equally. Point by point __________ is a good feature to =
incorporate into a=20
model Muslim civilization in BC because ___________. If Arab-based =
(Mecca-based)=20
civilization is the best of the best, prove it. Prove it here in Canada, =

peacefully. Prove that the Muslim repudiation of the God of the Bible is =
correct=20
and that all nations shall be blessed in it more than Israel. BC has =
room for=20
many future cities. It is twice the area of Japan. When the gates are =
open will=20
migrating people of the world flock into a Muslim city, a Catholic city, =

a=20
Buddhist city, a _______ city?</FONT></DIV>
<DIV><FONT size=3D2 face=3DArial></FONT> </DIV>
<DIV><FONT size=3D2 face=3DArial>It only requires
Muslim CANOPOLIS =
contestants to=20
complete the sentence ___________ is a good feature of
a Muslim =
CANOPOLIS=20
because ________________ in accordance with the
definition of =
=E2=80=9Cgood=E2=80=9D in Koran=20
75:13, =E2=80=9CThe Resurrection=E2=80=9D which says,
=E2=80=9CThen man =
will be told what he had sent=20
ahead (of good) and what he had left behind=E2=80=9D.
Will the Muslim =
CANOPOLIS be the=20
=E2=80=9Cbest of the best=E2=80=9D among scores or
perhaps hundreds of =
future reservations in=20
Canada? Will it be the model of =E2=80=9Cpeace, order
and good =
government=E2=80=9D? Will the=20
American CANOPOLIS declare that =E2=80=9CWhen America
ceased to be good =
it ceased to be=20
great .... until it discovered the goodness of
Islam=E2=80=9D? Does the =
Muslim CANOPOLIS=20
Constitution begin with, =E2=80=9CWhereas Muslim
CANOPOLIS is founded =
upon principles=20
that recognize the supremacy of Allah =
___________________________=E2=80=9D?</FONT></DIV>
<DIV><FONT size=3D2 face=3DArial></FONT> </DIV>
<DIV><FONT size=3D2 face=3DArial>ASK THE
EXPERTS!</FONT></DIV>
<DIV><FONT size=3D2 face=3DArial></FONT> </DIV>
<DIV><FONT size=3D2 face=3DArial><STRONG><U>CHAPTER
13:</U></STRONG> =
<STRONG>CHINESE=20
CANADIAN CIVILIZATION</STRONG></FONT></DIV>
<DIV><STRONG><FONT size=3D2
face=3DArial></FONT></STRONG> </DIV>
<DIV><FONT color=3D#0000ff size=3D2
face=3DArial><STRONG>There is =

```
something formed of=20
chaos,</STRONG></FONT></DIV>
<DIV><FONT color=3D#0000ff size=3D2
face=3DArial><STRONG>Born before =
heaven and=20
earth,</STRONG></FONT></DIV>
<DIV><FONT color=3D#0000ff size=3D2
face=3DArial><STRONG>Silent and =
void, it is not=20
renewed.</STRONG></FONT></DIV>
<DIV><FONT color=3D#0000ff size=3D2
face=3DArial><STRONG>It goes on =
forever without=20
failing.</STRONG></FONT></DIV>
<DIV><FONT size=3D2 face=3DArial></FONT> </DIV>
<DIV><FONT size=3D2 face=3DArial>- Tao Te
Ching</FONT></DIV>
<DIV><FONT size=3D2 face=3DArial></FONT> </DIV>
<DIV><FONT size=3D2 face=3DArial></FONT> <FONT
face=3DCalibri>What =
color should=20
be used for the words above from the Tao Te Ching? Why?
<STRONG><U><FONT =

color=3D#ff0000>In China, red is the color of
celebration, the color of =
good news=20
which is Gospel news.</FONT></U></STRONG> China towns
are popular in =
Canada. Why=20
not a China City of 100,000? And what
ideology/religion/belief system =
should it=20
use for the CANOPOLIS Constitution? </FONT><FONT
face=3DCalibri>Consider =
the=20
twins, Happy Nappy Ho of the CIA (Chinese Intelligence
Agency) and Nappy =
Happy=20
Ho of the CIA (Canadian Intelligence Agency) ... or is
it vice-versa? =
Tell us a=20
Tale Of Two Chinese cities for the CANOPOLIS
constitutional contest. =
China is a=20
multireligious country and in that sense it is
multicultural. Xinjiang, =
```

the=20
largest province in area adjoins Pakistan and links to Gilgit Province =
in=20
Pakistan by the Karakorum Highway which is one of the wonders of the =
modern=20
world. Xinjiang religion is mostly Muslim. The highest Karakorum pass is =
above=20
most clouds at three miles. Fine ice crystals fall instead of rain. =
BC=E2=80=99s highest=20
mountain (Robson) is only about two miles above sea level. The tree line =
in BC=20
is at one mile. Above that we look up to our mountains and see bare =
rock.=20
</FONT></DIV>
<DIV><FONT face=3DCalibri></FONT> </DIV>
<DIV><FONT face=3DCalibri>China has a historic benefit when it comes to =
thinking=20
about Moon civilization because millions of people still live in =
mountain caves.=20
Not only is there a problem of radiation from space for those living on =
the Moon=20
but there is also a problem of rocks in all sizes falling from the sky =
since it=20
contains almost no atmosphere to vaporize even the smallest stone. One=20
bean-sized rock could be deadly. A survey of Chinese troglodyte culture =
by Nappy=20
and Nappy would be a good start. For example, south exposure would =
probably be=20
preferred in China and that means a sunny location on the Moon is best. =
Darker=20
and cooler places are found when colonists tunnel into rock. There are =
health=20

problems associated with mineral content as is the case
for =
asbestos-family=20
minerals and minerals which are highly radioactive.
Mental health =
problems are=20
also linked to claustrophobia and excessive darkness as
well as poor air =

circulation (stale air).</FONT></DIV>
<DIV><FONT face=3DCalibri></FONT> </DIV>
<DIV><FONT face=3DCalibri>What of Chinese CANOPOLIS
religion? The CIA is =
fully=20
aware that Xinjiang is almost the only troubled region
in China at the =
time of=20
this writing and the Muslim provinces bordering India
and Pakistan are =
almost=20
the only troubled region for India where the
world=E2=80=99s biggest =
infantry face-off=20
exists (comparable to Eastern-Western European face-
offs during World =
War 2 and=20
Cold War). The CIA is not fooled into thinking that the
Muslim religion =
has=20
nothing to do with this though propagandizing media in
general would =
have us=20
believe that the global terrorism epidemic is brought
to us by people =
who =E2=80=9Cjust=20
happen to be Muslims=E2=80=9D. The CANOPOLIS Contest
requires that the =
connection=20
between beliefs and practices is made
clear.</FONT></DIV>
<DIV><FONT face=3DCalibri></FONT> </DIV>
<DIV><FONT face=3DCalibri>Nappy Happy Ho can text in
the winning =
CANOPOLIS essay=20
along with a new Canadian flag with the red removed ...
or will it be =
Happy=20

Nappy Ho whose flag has the white removed?</FONT></DIV>
<DIV><FONT size=3D2 face=3DArial></FONT> </DIV>
<DIV><FONT size=3D2 face=3DArial><STRONG><U>CHAPTER 14:
</U><FONT =
color=3D#000000>THE=20
INEFFABLE CANADIAN </FONT></STRONG></FONT></DIV>
<DIV><FONT size=3D2 face=3DArial></FONT> </DIV>
<DIV><FONT size=3D2 face=3DArial><STRONG><FONT
color=3D#ff0000 =
size=3D3>I am the root=20
and the offspring of David, and the bright and morning
=
star</FONT></STRONG> -=20
Revelation 22:16</FONT></DIV>
<DIV><FONT size=3D2 face=3DArial></FONT> </DIV>
<DIV><FONT size=3D2 face=3DArial>The late, great
psychiatrist K =
Dabrowski was a=20
faculty member at the University of Alberta. His theory
of "positive=20
disintegration" as he called it put forward the idea
that social and=20
psychological disintegration often precedes a positive
re-integration =
for the=20
better. This is in keeping with the words of TJWSHWG
that unless a seed =
falls to=20
the ground it cannot grow. The uncoupling of BC from
Canada is firstly a =

disintegration of Canada but the resulting
reintegration will take =
Canada=20
forward ad astra. This is the fruition of decades of
large scale =
immigration and=20
multiculturalism and the nationwide cure of xenophobia.
Imagine BC with =
double=20
the population of Japan. With twice the area of Japan
and a friendly =
competition=20
between the dozen or so major First Nation groupings
for personnel =
resources, a=20
population in the hundreds of millions is sustainable,

especially as =
minerals=20
and power are exported back to BC from colonies on Moon,
Mars and =
beyond. To=20
give an idea of the magnitude of these resources,
consider what Yeomans =
writes=20
in Chapter 7 of his "Near-Earth Objects" book. Chapter
7 is titled =
:Nature's=20
Natural Resources and the Human Exploration of our
Solar System". He =
notes that=20
even a lower grade and not so large rocky asteroid may
contain trillions =
of=20
dollars worth of metals. There are thousands of these
asteroids on the =
Moon.=20
</FONT></DIV>
<DIV><FONT size=3D2 face=3DArial></FONT> </DIV>
<DIV><FONT size=3D2 face=3DArial>Positive reintegration
of BC as the =
sovereign and=20
independent entity it legally has been all along will
allow Canada to =
spell out=20
its model of Canadian ideals and submit them to lawful
First Nation BC=20
authorities. After so many years of multiculturalism,
the MPs and =
Senators of=20
Ottawa must have clear ideas about which features of
those various =
cultures are=20
the best of the best contrasted with those which are
regressive and=20
harmful. Positive disintegration does not mean
termination or=20
extermination. Faith without works is dead. That
popular statement =
is=20
derived from the catechism of all catechisms, the Bible.
In CC p 170 we =
read=20
"The believer's act (of faith) does not terminate in

the propositions =
but in the=20
realities (which they express)". What is the Canadian =
reality?</FONT></DIV>
<DIV><FONT size=3D2 face=3DArial></FONT> </DIV>
<DIV><FONT size=3D2 face=3DArial>Shallow political-
judicial jingoisms =
and slogans do=20
not constitute integrity. Political-judicial actors on
stage can =
skillfully be=20
imitated by Hollywood or Bollywood actors. The same can
be said for =
simulations=20
of religiosity, piety and holiness. Movies like Oh God,
Almighty Bruce, =
Oh My=20
God (Bollywood), Angels and Demons, Apparitions
(BBC) and others =
prove=20
this so well. Angels and Demons (Ron Howard producer)
presents the =
circumstance=20
of an impostor pope putting himself forward as the King
of Rome on the =
Throne of=20
Christ which is not in itself such an extreme
possibility. The Roman =
Catholic=20
religion has formally identified some two dozen such
impostors over the =
past=20
2,000 years. What then differentiates true Romanist
civilization from an =

impostor?</FONT></DIV>
<DIV><FONT size=3D2 face=3DArial></FONT> </DIV>
<DIV><FONT size=3D2 face=3DArial>A Judahite core of
civilization rose =
up,=20
Phoenix-like from the ashen circumstances of the
torture and murder of =
Jesus=20
Christ. TJWSHWG makes the point by apologetics that to
create this as a =
fiction=20
or fable which people will then immediately adhere to

even at the cost =
of their=20
lives is almost impossible. Where are the "creative
writers" today to =
show how=20
it could have been done? Even the imaginative BBC
cannot do this. The=20
ecclesiastical history of the Bible gives some
numbers. There were =
120 of=20
the faithful at the beginning of Acts who probably
studied with Jesus =
Christ,=20
the Torah personified post-resurrection and pre-
ascencion and =
subsequently Acts=20
presents repeated reference to "thousands" of new
adherents There were =
500+ in a=20
"brotherhood" who claimed to have witnessed the miracle
of all miracles, =
the=20
resurrection of TJWSHWG. These were the hundreds and
the thousands of =
Jews who=20
did not find the perfect offering of Jesus to be a
stumbling block and =
by cruel=20
irony of history their descendants today are denied
right of return to =
Israel=20
while atheists in large numbers are admitted. But the
superiority of =
this=20
Judahite civilization today can become that p 170
reality in =
BC.</FONT></DIV>
<DIV><FONT size=3D2 face=3DArial></FONT> </DIV>
<DIV><FONT size=3D2 face=3DArial>Canadian nationalism
is not so shallow =
to consist=20
of lines on a map. Look at the geopolitical maps of
history. The change =
in=20
border boundaries is enormous. Many nations have
disappeared by name. =
New=20

nations have arisen. The UN has only about 200 members.
But the number =
of=20
national groupings who could be members is in the
thousands. Where is =
the Basque=20
nation in the UN General Assembly? Ireland, once part
of UK has a seat. =
Where is=20
the UN delegate of Scotland? Will nations in space be
offshoots of =
nations on=20
this planet or will they create new national entities?
Canadianism is =
idealism=20
in search of actualization. BC, liberated from a
fraudulent natural =
resource=20
grab by the greedy of Ottawa in 1871 can give
Canadianism that reality.=20
</FONT></DIV>
<DIV><FONT size=3D2 face=3DArial></FONT> </DIV>
<DIV><FONT size=3D2 face=3DArial>The New Canada will
truly be a DOMAIN =
and in that=20
sense merits a new name as so many nations have now
renamed themselves. =
One=20
possibility is <FONT color=3D#c0504d><EM><U><STRONG>The
Domain of=20
Canada</STRONG>.</U></EM></FONT> This denotes the
rebirth of a=20
spiritually/ideologically born-again Canada which
fairly embraces all =
cultures=20
equally <U>in just competition</U> without the current
pathetically =
inadequate=20
Charter s15 interpretation that we get from
=E2=80=9CNew World =
Order=E2=80=9D sycophants in the=20
political-judicial system. Such people flee like
cockroaches when the =
light of=20
good, honest questions impinges on their pathetic
exercises in casuistry =
applied=20

to the hundreds of religions and the hundreds of sexual
orientations in =
this=20
world. They are not all equal in fact but they are
equally entitled to =
compete.=20
The New Canadian is still as ineffable as the (somewhat
tongue-in-cheek) =
CIA of=20
Chapter 13 and its =E2=80=9Ccosmological top
secret=E2=80=9D projects. =
By the time Japan, Russia=20
et al are building their Moon colonies which is
expected to be 2030, the =
New=20
Canadian will emerge from the darkness of the current
political-judicial =
system.=20
This one-party system was called NDP
(NoDamnedPrinciples) or =
=E2=80=9CParty of the=20
Trough=E2=80=9D in Gold War. Arguably Deputy Prime
Minister Nielsen =
understated when he=20
called Parliament a den of liars and FLQ leader
Vallieres likewise =
understated=20
when he wrote =E2=80=9CWhite Niggers=E2=80=9D. Future
Canada is much =
brighter than those=20
writings convey.</FONT></DIV>
<DIV><FONT size=3D2 face=3DArial></FONT> </DIV>
<DIV><FONT size=3D2 face=3DArial>ASK THE
EXPERTS!</FONT></DIV>
<DIV><FONT size=3D2 face=3DArial></FONT> </DIV>
<DIV><FONT size=3D2 face=3DArial><STRONG><U>CHAPTER 15:
</U>TRUE LOVE =
AND CANADIAN=20
PARLIAMENTARY CATECHISM</STRONG></FONT></DIV>
<DIV><FONT size=3D2 face=3DArial></FONT> </DIV>
<DIV><FONT size=3D2 face=3DArial><STRONG><FONT
color=3D#ff0000 =
size=3D3>Love God with=20
all your heart and soul and mind and
strength</FONT></STRONG> - Mark=20
12:29</FONT></DIV>
<DIV><FONT size=3D2 face=3DArial></FONT> </DIV>

```
<DIV><FONT size=3D2 face=3DArial>JW Woodside's Foreward
to the Divine =
services Book=20
For The Canadian Armed Forces (1950) says "This book is
designed to meet =
the=20
religious needs of the men and women in the various
branches of the =
Forces".=20
Today, a multicultural/multireligious Canada must face
the reality that =
all=20
religions have the constitutional right to equality
(Charter section 15) =
which=20
means each has the equal right to prove that its WAY OF
LIFE is "the =
best of the=20
best". It does not mean that all religions are
inherently equal. When =
God is=20
defined as =E2=80=9Cthe best of the best=E2=80=9D and
the source of all =
blessings who can confer=20
them on any of us, even the Atheist can accept the Mark
12:29=20
citation.</FONT></DIV>
<DIV><FONT size=3D2 face=3DArial></FONT> </DIV>
<DIV><FONT size=3D2 face=3DArial>The Canadian
political-judicial system =
has no=20
jurisdiction over natural resources in British Columbia.
It is ultra =
vires.=20
Personnel or human resources are another matter. As
First Nations of BC =
take=20
their places in the UN General Assembly over the next
century, leases =
like the=20
now-expired Hong Kong lease can be negotiated between
these personnel, =
their MP=20
and Senate representatives, and Canada. The new
immigration policy of BC =
will be=20
in First Nation hands, empowered by new-found precious
```

metal discoveries =
in the=20
trillions of dollars as "Gold War" predicts. Religion
is merely an act =
which=20
Hollywood, Bollywood and BBC actors simulate with ease
unless it is =
translated=20
into a comprehensive way of life, 24/7. Canada must
concede that the =
Indian=20
people of BC have never given up their natural resource
rights. It is =
not a=20
matter of "giving them back". They never belonged to
Canada. What will=20
concentrated populations of human resources nested
within BC Indian =
nations=20
yield? Which is "the best of the best"?</FONT></DIV>
<DIV><FONT size=3D2 face=3DArial></FONT> </DIV>
<DIV><FONT size=3D2 face=3DArial>A $5,000 advance on
royalties for CCCC =
(Catholic=20
Catechism Critique Corrected) was offered in Catholic
Catechism Critique =

(Friesen) and NEWTOWN (Kindle).</FONT></DIV>
<DIV><FONT size=3D2 face=3DArial></FONT> </DIV>
<DIV><FONT size=3D2 face=3DArial>This offer is in
accord with the GODBOT =

presentation above. <STRONG><U>GODBOT is first a =
grammarian</U></STRONG>. If=20
experts in religious doctrine or teaching mastery at
Catholic and =
Protestant=20
universities in particular are not eager to come
forward to the light of =
day=20
before billions of people now text-machine connected
and correct what =
some will=20
see as a heresy, why not? Do they not understand the
Golden Rule? I =
correct you=20
and you correct me. If they are by contrast not willing

to come forward =
and=20
proclaim it a breakthrough in religious analysis and
understanding, why =
not? The=20
Israelite Magisterium and Torah defined as sacred
teaching tradition (De =
Sola=20
Pool) </FONT><FONT size=3D2 face=3DArial>calls for us
to "love good and =
hate evil"=20
and thus we, like King David "hate those who hate Thee
(God) with a =
perfect=20
hatred". Who is the God of the Canadian Constitution?
"Whereas Canada is =
founded=20
upon the supremacy of God ____________"? God is love
says the Gospel of=20
John. But we have an expression in English
vernacular: TRUE LOVE. =
Does=20
Parliament love evil? The United Nations is little more
than a debating =
club for=20
rich and powerful despots, many being the concentrated
evil of humankind =

(although Indian nation entry will have symbolic value
pertaining to =
recognition=20
of autonomy). Is Parliament mostly likewise ... a
debating club for=20
men/women/other driven by ego and greed? Does it have
the expertise to =
welcome a=20
political-religious catechism of good, honest questions
and good, honest =

answers? Can it spell out on the blank screens of
GODBOT, a computer in =
humanoid=20
form, that which is both good and true? Or do we say
that Parliament =
loves evil=20
and hates good which seems to be the theme of the
perversely bad BBC =

series=20
"Misfits"? Can the English Parliament even analyze
"Misfits" without =
groveling=20
before the twisted English deity of political
correctness? Can they =
"talk about=20
what the English are not supposed to talk about" or do
we say the modern =
English=20
parliamentarian is too much the liar and coward to do
so? </FONT><FONT =
size=3D2=20
face=3DArial>Are the Red Letter words of Revelation
21:8 a description =
of the=20
future King Charles as head of the Church of England?
Obviously TJWSHWG =
did not=20
come to save us from the first death but those who
commit themselves to =
lies=20
rather than Him are not saved from the second death we
read in Rev 21:8. =
"Every=20
time I look into the Holy Book I want to tremble" sings
Canadian folk =
singer Ann=20
Murray. If King Charles assisted by all of his bishops
and =
parliamentarians=20
cannot tell BBC or GODBOT the difference between true
love and false =
love, can=20
the Canadian Parliament help him out? "Misfits" seems
designed by those =
who love=20
twisted perversity, sexually and otherwise. The English
ship of state is =
lost at=20
sea. Canada's Parliament can do better than that and
guide them to safe=20
harbor.</FONT></DIV>
<DIV><FONT size=3D2 face=3DArial></FONT> </DIV>
<DIV><FONT size=3D2 face=3DArial>ASK THE
EXPERTS!</FONT></DIV>
<DIV><FONT size=3D2 face=3DArial></FONT> </DIV>

<DIV><FONT size=3D2 =
face=3DArial><STRONG><U>CLOSING</U></STRONG></FONT></DI
V>
<DIV><FONT size=3D2 face=3DArial></FONT> </DIV>
<DIV><FONT size=3D2 face=3DArial></FONT> </DIV>
<DIV><FONT size=3D2 face=3DArial><STRONG><FONT
color=3D#ff0000 =
size=3D3>And many false=20
prophets shall arise, and deceive many</FONT></STRONG>
- Matthew=20
24:11</FONT></DIV>
<DIV><FONT size=3D2 face=3DArial></FONT> </DIV>
<DIV><FONT size=3D2 face=3DArial>What are the words of
the prophets? =
Sometimes they=20
are written on the subway walls as Simon and Garfunkel
say. Sometimes =
they are=20
written on the hard drives and thumb drives of GODBOT
teaching machines. =
How=20
would a Xulon Press God Tube interview with GODBOT at
Notre Dame's God =
Quad play=20
out? What questions about Catholic Catechism would the
Xulon interviewer =
as=20
expert representative ask GODBOT and the Notre Dame
professors? What =
questions=20
would self-proclaimed religion experts pronounce
anathema or heretical =
even=20
though they are important matters of life and death in
the public =
domain? An=20
Internet search on religious honorifics and titles
reveals an =
astonishing=20
plethora of self-aggrandizing vanities. If this self-
proclaimed =
holiness,=20
divinity, piety and revered status is more than vanity
they will be =
eager to=20
come forward and prove their expertise about how we
should live on this =

planet=20
and beyond. Otherwise, the Biblical assertion that
there is none =
righteous, no=20
not one, with related passages stand firm. The world is
awash in =
religious=20
fraud. The Catholic Catechism paragraph 801 testing of
all things is =
easily=20
applied to Catholic catechizers. Deceivers who run away
at Notre Dame =
and=20
elsewhere prove who they serve by such
testing.</FONT></DIV>
<DIV><FONT size=3D2 face=3DArial></FONT> </DIV>
<DIV><FONT size=3D2 face=3DArial>Some of these moral
matters are =
technologically=20
disguised. Space age technologies can save many lives.
Does "Thou shalt =
not=20
kill" ring the proverbial bell? Modern technology can
export =
transportation=20
systems which rarely take a human life. The city core
of Vancouver on =
the other=20
hand </FONT><FONT size=3D2 face=3DArial>takes about 30
lives per year in =
vehicular=20
accidents. The post-traumatic disorders afflicted upon
family, friends =
and even=20
police and other first responders may not heal in a
life time. Do the =
religion=20
experts want sclerotic, life-destroying transportation
technology =
exported to=20
the Canadian Moon? Consider the "flying train" of
Robert Goddard, dubbed =
the=20
progenitor of American rocket science. It was he who
first proposed what =
is=20
today called the hyperloop in California, about to be

built by Hyperloop =

Transportation Technology Inc. and not robophobe
billionaire, Elon Musk =
despite=20
what he might claim in bragging rights. Goddard
patented the idea of a =
vacuum or=20
near-vacuum tube with a train which could attain up to
space speeds. It =
is about=20
to be tested in California by Hyperloop Transportation
Technology Inc =
which has=20
also inked a deal with land owners for the
track.</FONT></DIV>
<DIV><FONT size=3D2 face=3DArial></FONT> </DIV>
<DIV><FONT size=3D2 face=3DArial>Bombardier Canada
technologies on the =
Moon will use=20
Goddard ideas which hybridize the plane and the train.
The magnetic =
levitation=20
train or mag-lev is in effect a plane-train combination.
It is a flying =
train.=20
On the Moon it needs no vacuum tube. Because of the low
gravity as well, =
flying=20
trains could be propelled from the Moon into space
perhaps with =
mountains like=20
the Mountain of Eternal Light as launch ramps.
Bombardier which is =
sometimes=20
government subsidized, is Canada's leading
transportation technology =
expert. The=20
company describes itself as NUMBER ONE GLOBALLY in the
manufacture and =
sale of=20
trains and planes in combination. It could even create
the CANOPOLIS=20
transportation system here in BC, first on paper. Since
Bombardier =
receives=20
government funding, it would be appropriate for

Parliament to ask it for =
plans=20
to a CANOPOLIS transportation system which would meet
the criteria of =
"little or=20
no pollution" and "few, if any, fatalities". Integrated
technologies =
would range=20
from moving sidewalks to sky trains (like the one
operating since 1986 =
with an=20
almost perfect safety record) to interplanetary plane-
train=20
hybrids.</FONT></DIV>
<DIV><FONT size=3D2 face=3DArial></FONT> </DIV>
<DIV><FONT size=3D2 face=3DArial>Words have to be put
into practice. The =
words of=20
the Bible in and of themselves have no meaning. They
are only atoms and=20
molecules fashioned into ink, computer screen markings
and so on as =
stated=20
repeatedly in earlier chapters. GODBOT is a machine
tabula rasa until=20
political-religious experts revive the catechism genre
of literature and =
prove=20
otherwise. BC can send a GODBOT to Library of
Parliament to serve as =
chief=20
librarian. Perhaps it will be built by lely.com or its
=
westcoastrobotics.com=20
branch in BC as an "astronaut" model. It will walk and
talk like ASIMO =
or NAO.=20
This will be a $6,000,000 humanoid. That is a fair
price tag. When will =
it be=20
delivered?</FONT></DIV>
<DIV><FONT size=3D2 face=3DArial></FONT> </DIV>
<DIV><FONT size=3D2 face=3DArial>ASK THE
EXPERTS!</FONT></DIV>
<DIV><FONT size=3D2 face=3DArial></FONT> </DIV>
<DIV><FONT size=3D2 face=3DArial>Rock
Hunter</FONT></DIV>

```
<DIV><FONT size=3D2 face=3DArial>Sto:lo Nation, British
Columbia, =
2016</FONT></DIV>
<DIV><FONT size=3D2 face=3DArial></FONT> </DIV>
<DIV><FONT size=3D2 face=3DArial></FONT> </DIV>
<DIV><FONT size=3D2 =
face=3DArial><STRONG><U>EXCURSUS</U></STRONG></FONT></D
IV>
<DIV><FONT size=3D2 face=3DArial></FONT> </DIV>
<DIV><FONT face=3DArial></FONT> </DIV>
<DIV><FONT size=3D2 face=3DArial><FONT color=3D#ff0000
=
size=3D3><STRONG>And he that=20
hateth his life in this world shall keep it unto life =
eternal</STRONG><FONT=20
color=3D#000000 size=3D2> - John
12:25</FONT></FONT></FONT></DIV>
<DIV><FONT size=3D2 face=3DArial></FONT> </DIV>
<DIV><FONT size=3D2 face=3DArial>What if we use this
emphasis: He that =
hateth his=20
life in THIS world __________? Catholic Catechism says
in paragraph 2,852 =
that=20
"the whole world is in the power of the evil one". Does
that not mean =
both=20
institutions of church and state? Does that mean we
must export an =
equally evil=20
model of the civilization which is "in this world" off-
planet? =
</FONT><FONT=20
size=3D2 face=3DArial>If religious people at Notre Dame,
the Curia in =
Rome and among=20
the thousands of Xulon and Friesen contributors are not
always "in the =
power of=20
the evil one" should they not be EAGER to come forward
and tell the =
world about=20
their shining city on a hill, their CANOPOLIS, worthy
of export to Moon, =
Mars=20
and beyond? <STRONG><FONT color=3D#000000><U>If life in
THIS world is =
```

justifiably=20
hated, emigrate to another
world</U></FONT></STRONG>.</FONT></DIV>
<DIV><FONT size=3D2 face=3DArial></FONT> </DIV>
<DIV><FONT size=3D2 face=3DArial>What should it be like?
ASK THE =
EXPERTS! Those=20
experts in academia who cannot use first person
Socratic dialogue (or =
its=20
eastern equivalent) to engage GODBOT in the many
necessary questions are =
not=20
truly learned people. They are just pinheads. What
questions should =
three wise=20
men of the west like the =E2=80=9Cthree amigos=E2=80=9D,
Trump, Ventura =
and Black ask GODBOT?=20
How would they differ from the questions of three wise
men of the east =
who went=20
to Judea to meet =E2=80=9CThe King of the
Jews=E2=80=9D?</FONT></DIV>
<DIV><FONT size=3D2 face=3DArial></FONT> </DIV>
<DIV><FONT size=3D2 face=3DArial>The GODBOT script
above was written =
with the=20
intention of being as objective as the rain which falls
on the just and =
the=20
unjust concerning scientific and technological
possibilities. But this =
in no way=20
condones moral or cultural relativity or "new age"
doctrine defined by=20
quasi-religious ideology which tries to turn fiction
and superstition =
into fact=20
as a foundation for choices in life.</FONT><FONT
size=3D2 =
face=3DArial>This=20
impartial objectivity was not always adhered to but the
GODBOT writing =
stance=20
was a way of inviting experts from all fields to make
their =

contributions toward=20
Future Canada. This Excursus is an advocacy of
accepting BIBLICAL TRUTH =
as a=20
foundation for all belief and thus non-believers are
fairly warned of =
the=20
material which follows. BIBLICAL TRUTH can only be
comprehended Sola =
Gracia.=20
Only guided by the Holy Spirit of God, meaning Absolute
Truth can the =
Bible be=20
understood. This reality</FONT><FONT size=3D2
face=3DArial> generalizes. =
Only if we=20
are guided by TRUTH will be able to understand ANY
writing or even a=20
non-writing, a blank page. Only guided by TRUTH can we
understand any=20
communication, including the information communicated
by nature. The =
following=20
reasoning is deliberately circular. <STRONG><U>The
Bible is the inerrant =
word of=20
God because the inerrant word of God is the =
Bible</U></STRONG>.</FONT></DIV>
<DIV><FONT size=3D2 face=3DArial></FONT> </DIV>
<DIV><FONT size=3D2 face=3DArial>The writer's belief
system is solidly =
founded upon=20
the Trinitarian Apostles' Creed. No apology is made for
that. This Creed =
is the=20
monotheistic light of Judaism carried forward by the
nation of Judah =
under Roman=20
occupation. The Old Testament is not merely a book (or
collection of =
books)=20
about God. It is a book by God. God is speaking to man
throughout this =
book.=20
Those words are His Red Letter words. Black letter
words are commentary, =

analysis, reflection and so on as they pertain to what God is saying. =
Witnesses,=20
reporters, writers are the people who have a secondary role to this =
Authorship.=20
Expert Bible scholars can comment on HOW those Red Letter words are =
expressed.=20
Two sensory modalities only are mentioned in the Bible - sight and sound =
(voice)=20
with touch being a rare exception (Thomas touched the wound of Jesus).=20
<U><STRONG>God is seen and heard</STRONG></U>. The language spoken by =
God must=20
have been understandable to recipients who spoke different languages. =
The=20
Hebrew-Eberic languages changed greatly over hundreds and thousands of =
years.=20
Otherwise, no clarification of God's language is given in the Bible. =
What=20
language was used in the early sections of Genesis which were long =
before any=20
Hebrew language? What language did God use to speak to Adam and Eve? How =
does=20
the Hebrew which He presumably spoke to Jacob/Israel or Moses compare to =
the=20
Hebrew used in Israel today? What language did Jesus speak in the =
Gospels? Did=20
He speak to the learned religious leaders using the Hebrew of the day or =
the=20
Hebrew of Jacob/Israel or the Hebrew of Moses? Did He speak to the =
crowds in=20
Aramaic and Romans like Pilate in Latin? What is the meaning of God's=20
multilingual miracle in Chapter 2 of Acts,

communicating to the devout =
Jews out=20
of every nation under heaven?</FONT></DIV>
<DIV><FONT size=3D2 face=3DArial></FONT> </DIV>
<DIV><FONT size=3D2 face=3DArial>The Bible, Sola Gracia
can only be =
understood as a=20
series of questionable statements. Did TJWSHWG ever
turn away a good, =
honest=20
question? Since God does not want us to be deceived by
impostors, surely =
He=20
wants us to ask lots of good, honest questions to the
catechizers of all =

religions and thus find out who the wolves in
sheep=E2=80=99s' clothing =
are. For=20
example, when we read Koran, 2:85-87 "Remember We gave
Moses the Book =
and sent=20
after him many an apostle; and to Jesus, son of Mary,
We gave clear =
evidence of=20
the truth". </FONT><FONT size=3D2 face=3DArial>Who =3D
"We" in this =
passage? Who =3D "I"=20
in Chapter 75 which is titled "The Resurrection"? It is
not Allah =
because this=20
unnamed =E2=80=9CI=E2=80=9D is said in that chapter to
be speaking in =
the name of Allah. And=20
thus "When will the Day of Resurrection be?" (75:6) and
who will define =
the=20
=E2=80=9Cgood=E2=80=9D deeds of 75:13 which speak for a
favorable =
resurrection? Since Classical=20
Arabic is read by very few today, which of these
readers decides what =
the words=20
We and I mean in this context or what anything in Koran
means? Or does =
that=20
"Numero Uno" position among readers falls to someone

today who is not =
familiar=20
with Classical Arabic? Who constitutes the
=E2=80=9CMagisterium=E2=80=9D =
of Islam? Would that=20
seniormost position of reader/interpreter also mean the
reader is most =
senior to=20
serve as WRITER of the GODBOT C program? Space is left
here for a C =
program as=20
the GOBDOT pages in RAM and hard drive are blank. You
and the experts =
must write=20
them. Catechizing wolves of all belief systems in
sheep=E2=80=99s =
clothing will run away=20
from the truth which shines from good, honest questions.
They are the =
liars=20
and/or cowards of Revelation 21:8 whose eternity after
the second death =
is=20
surely hellish if they are committed to the lies.
</FONT><FONT size=3D2=20
face=3DArial>Is there any so-called Christian teaching
institution which =
can=20
describe a Christian CANOPOLIS compared to a Muslim
CANOPOLIS or shall =
we say=20
that today=E2=80=99s religious teaching institutions
are frauds against =
both God and=20
man?</FONT></DIV>
<DIV><FONT size=3D2 face=3DArial></FONT> </DIV>
<DIV><FONT size=3D2 face=3DArial>The medium is not the
message. Many =
questions may=20
be asked about the medium for Red Letter words. A few
details are given =
in the=20
Bible. Nature may be cited as a medium (for example the
whirlwind by =
which God=20
spoke to Job) and natural phenomena, often dramatic,
like lightning and =

great=20
storms and fire, may accompany the Red Letter words. Are these not part =
of the=20
language of God - a non-verbal language? What are the limits on this =
language of=20
performance? Given that God is all-powerful, there is no theoretical =
limit. God=20
can use GODBOT as a medium IHS (In His Service).</FONT></DIV>
<DIV><FONT size=3D2 face=3DArial></FONT> </DIV>
<DIV><FONT size=3D2 face=3DArial>We are all familiar with the saying, =
"an act of=20
God". All acts must be either directly or indirectly acts of God since =
God is=20
all powerful. What do the experts in religion and theology say about =
evil acts?=20
What do we read in Genesis 3:22 and Isaiah 45:7? Since God=E2=80=99s =
power is=20
immeasurably above ours, there are times when He says, Do as I say and =
not as I=20
do. Evil as well as good are His responsibility. There is no instance in =
the=20
Bible of Red Letter words which tell humans to perpetrate evil. What do =
the=20
experts say of the cruelty in nature? Is it good or evil or neither? A =
child's=20
hymn says: "This is my Father's world ... He speaks to me everywhere".=20
</FONT><FONT size=3D2 face=3DArial>Is every act or expression in nature =
a Red Letter=20
expression? Canadian folksinger Gordon Lightfoot sings "Does anyone know =
where=20
the love of God goes?" ("The Wreck of the Edmund Fitzgerald"). And what =

do we=20
read in Matthew 27:46? "Eli, Eli, lama sabachthani?" God has dual =
responsibility=20
for good and evil but man is directed only to do good. CANOPOLIS and =
GODBOT are=20
about peace, order and good government.</FONT></DIV>
<DIV><FONT size=3D2 face=3DArial></FONT> </DIV>
<DIV><FONT size=3D2 face=3DArial>Red Letters of the Bible advocate only =
the=20
expression of good over evil and some will say this is utopianism. But =
God never=20
says, Do good only in limited places and at limited times. The Kingdom =
of Heaven=20
is advocated as a ideal which is to be turned into a reality on this =
planet=20
24/7. That ideal is pre-eminently why Jews and Romans colluded in =
deicide 2,000=20
years ago. The Roman emperor was self-deified and the Jews feared that =
they=20
would be ruthlessly persecuted if they announced that they must serve =
God rather=20
than man as is stated in Acts. Yet this is the Zionist ideal, found in =
every=20
book where God speaks to His Chosen People. Their beliefs were taught to =
the=20
entire world so Zionism became a global ideal. Babies born in Canada now =
can=20
expect to see colonies on Moon and Mars when they are adults. What kind =
of=20
CANOPOLIS will Canada export off-planet as the reality of this global=20
ideal?</FONT></DIV>
<DIV><FONT size=3D2 face=3DArial></FONT> </DIV>
<DIV><FONT color=3D#0000ff size=3D2

face=3DArial><STRONG>Russia is red, =
dilly=20
dilly;</STRONG></FONT></DIV>
<DIV><FONT color=3D#0000ff size=3D2
face=3DArial><STRONG>England is=20
green.</STRONG></FONT></DIV>
<DIV><FONT color=3D#0000ff size=3D2
face=3DArial><STRONG>We've got the =
Moon, dilly=20
dilly;</STRONG></FONT></DIV>
<DIV><FONT color=3D#0000ff size=3D2
face=3DArial><STRONG>They've got the =

Queen.</STRONG></FONT></DIV>
<DIV><FONT size=3D2 face=3DArial></FONT> </DIV>
<DIV><FONT size=3D2 face=3DArial>The Bible never says
to reject the =
natural laws. It=20
advocates REASONING and PROOF/TESTING. <STRONG><FONT
color=3D#ff0000 =
size=3D3>Let us=20
reason together ______</FONT></STRONG> What do we call
narrow-minded =
people=20
stuck in blind religious dogmas (or worse, dogmas which
are known to be =
false)?=20
We call them dogmatic bigots. What do we call academics
who reject the =
miracles=20
of Intelligent Design and Creation/Creative Science as
presented in the =
Bible=20
while accepting the miracles of quantum teleportation
and bilocation? =
They too=20
are dogmatic bigots.<U><STRONG><FONT color=3D#000000>
On the level of =
explanation=20
or theory neither Biblical miracles nor laboratory
quantum miracles =
=E2=80=9Cmake sense=E2=80=9D=20
because our minds are too limited to grasp the =
explanation</FONT></STRONG>.</U>=20
The lead actor in the movie, =E2=80=9CThe Life of
Pi=E2=80=9D is a Hindu =
who studies world=20

religions. Pi says the substitutionary atonement miracle whereby the =
blood of=20
Jesus pays for our sins =E2=80=9Cmakes no sense at all=E2=80=9D. Neither =
does quantum=20
teleportation make sense to any physicist. In both cases the facts are =
within=20
our grasp. What do we say of so-called Christians who reject good, =
honest=20
questions and answers in all manner of catechisms? C</FONT><FONT =
size=3D2=20
face=3DArial>hillingly <FONT color=3D#ff0000 size=3D3><FONT =
color=3D#000000 size=3D2>the=20
flock is</FONT><STRONG> small</STRONG></FONT> and straight is the gate, =
narrow=20
is the way and <STRONG><FONT color=3D#ff0000 =
size=3D3>few</FONT></STRONG> there be=20
that find it. Therefore, it is a miracle that there are those few who =
love=20
truth, who are wholly dedicated to truth, who are invited to seek and do =
find=20
this truth. </FONT></DIV>
<DIV><FONT size=3D2 face=3DArial></FONT> </DIV>
<DIV><FONT size=3D2 face=3DArial>It is irrefutable that the Holy Book =
declares truth=20
to be of two kinds: natural and super-natural. What then do we say of =
BC's=20
tourism slogan - "Super, Natural, BC"? BC WILL balkanize over this =
century.=20
Canada will accept that the 1871 colonialist seizure was an act of =
theft. Canada=20
will apologize to the First Nations of BC for ongoing genocide of those =
with=20
demographics like Frank Paul (poor/Indian/mentally ill)

which became a=20
nation-wide attack on the poor of all ethnicities. As a result of =
GODBOT's=20
never-ending Question Period (perhaps with a 5-13 robot ensconced at the =
Library=20
of Parliament) Canada will enter the era of space colonization and BC =
will lead=20
Canada after it is liberated from Ottawa colonialism. The seed which =
falls to=20
the ground will become the "Catechism Of The Future History Of New =
Canada" =20
according to a CANOPOLIS definition of civilization and of Canadian. =
These are=20
the Canadians who will travel to the Moon and some will live there =
indefinitely.=20
They will regard themselves as Moonlings. They will be our</FONT></DIV>
<DIV><FONT size=3D2 face=3DArial></FONT> </DIV>
<DIV><FONT size=3D2 face=3DArial>FUTURE
SAPIENS.</FONT></DIV>
<DIV><FONT size=3D2 face=3DArial></FONT> </DIV>
<DIV><FONT size=3D2 =
face=3DArial><STRONG><U>REFERENCES</U></STRONG></FONT><
/DIV>
<DIV><FONT size=3D2 face=3DArial></FONT> </DIV>
<DIV><FONT size=3D2 face=3DArial>Asimov, Isaac.
Asimov's Guide To The =
Bible: The Old=20
Testament, Avon Books, 1968</FONT></DIV>
<DIV><FONT size=3D2 face=3DArial></FONT> </DIV>
<DIV><FONT size=3D2 face=3DArial>Axworthy, Thomas S.
and Trudeau, Pierre =
Elliott=20
(Eds). Towards A Just Society: The Trudeau Years,
Viking, =
1990</FONT></DIV>
<DIV><FONT size=3D2 face=3DArial></FONT> </DIV>
<DIV><FONT size=3D2 face=3DArial>Catechism of the
Catholic Church. Pope =
John Paul II=20

(Karol Josef Wojtyla) edition, The Liturgical Press,
1994</FONT></DIV>
<DIV><FONT size=3D2 face=3DArial></FONT> </DIV>
<DIV><FONT size=3D2 face=3DArial>Catechism Of The
History Of =
Newfoundland. William=20
Charles, St John, Boston, GC Rand Printer,
1855</FONT></DIV>
<DIV><FONT size=3D2 face=3DArial></FONT> </DIV>
<DIV><FONT size=3D2 face=3DArial>Cyllorn, J. Stop
Apologizing, Procult =
Institute,=20
1991</FONT></DIV>
<DIV><FONT size=3D2 face=3DArial></FONT> </DIV>
<DIV><FONT size=3D2 face=3DArial>De Sola Pool (edition).
Traditional =
Jewish Prayer=20
Book, Behrman House, 1960</FONT></DIV>
<DIV><FONT size=3D2 face=3DArial></FONT> </DIV>
<DIV><FONT size=3D2 face=3DArial>Hunter, Rock. The Jew
Who Said He Was =
God=20
(TJWSHWG), Xulon Press, Florida, 2014; Library and
Archives Canada ISBN=20
978-0-9937593-0-7</FONT></DIV>
<DIV><FONT size=3D2 face=3DArial></FONT> </DIV>
<DIV><FONT size=3D2 face=3DArial>Hunter, Rock. Gold War:
The Lost Gold =
Mines Of=20
Canada's Mountain Indians, Xulon Press, Florida, 2015;
Library and =
Archives=20
Canada ISBN 978-0-9937593</FONT></DIV>
<DIV><FONT size=3D2 face=3DArial></FONT> </DIV>
<DIV><FONT size=3D2 face=3DArial>Hunter Rock, Catholic
Catechism =
Critique, Friesen=20
Press, 2015</FONT></DIV>
<DIV><FONT size=3D2 face=3DArial></FONT> </DIV>
<DIV><FONT size=3D2 face=3DArial>Hunter, Rock. NEWTOWN,
Kindle, =
2016</FONT></DIV>
<DIV><FONT size=3D2 face=3DArial></FONT> </DIV>
<DIV><FONT size=3D2 face=3DArial>Minister of National
Defence, Canada. =
Divine=20
Service Book, 1950</FONT></DIV>

<DIV><FONT size=3D2 face=3DArial></FONT> </DIV>
<DIV><FONT size=3D2 face=3DArial>Nielsen, Erik. The
House Is Not A Home, =
Macmillan,=20
1989</FONT></DIV>
<DIV><FONT size=3D2 face=3DArial></FONT> </DIV>
<DIV><FONT size=3D2 face=3DArial>Prata, Stephen. C
Primer Plus, Fourth =
Edition, Sams=20
Publishing, 2002</FONT></DIV>
<DIV><FONT size=3D2 face=3DArial></FONT> </DIV>
<DIV><FONT size=3D2 face=3DArial>Robinson, George.
Essential Judaism: A =
Complete=20
Guide To Beliefs, Customs and Rituals, Pocket Books,
2000</FONT></DIV>
<DIV><FONT size=3D2 face=3DArial></FONT> </DIV>
<DIV><FONT size=3D2 face=3DArial>Rosen, Jonathan. The
Talmud And The =
Internet,=20
Farrar, Straus and Giroux, 2000</FONT></DIV>
<DIV><FONT size=3D2 face=3DArial></FONT> </DIV>
<DIV><FONT size=3D2 face=3DArial>Sand, Shlomo. When And
How The Jewish =
People Was=20
Invented, published in Haaretz by Ofri
Ilani</FONT></DIV>
<DIV><FONT size=3D2 face=3DArial></FONT> </DIV>
<DIV><FONT size=3D2 face=3DArial>The Standard Jewish
Encyclopedia, =
1966</FONT></DIV>
<DIV><FONT size=3D2 face=3DArial></FONT> </DIV>
<DIV><FONT size=3D2 face=3DArial>Vallieres, Pierre.
White Niggers of =
America,=20
McClelland and Stewart, 1971</FONT></DIV>
<DIV><FONT size=3D2 face=3DArial></FONT> </DIV>
<DIV><FONT size=3D2 face=3DArial>Wilkerson, David. The
Jesus Person =
Pocket Promise=20
Book, Regal Books, 1972</FONT></DIV>
<DIV><FONT size=3D2 face=3DArial></FONT> </DIV>
<DIV><FONT size=3D2 face=3DArial>Wray, TJ. What The
Bible Really Tells =
Us: The=20
Essential Guide To Biblical Literacy, Rowman and
Littlefield, =

2011</FONT></DIV>
<DIV><FONT size=3D2 face=3DArial></FONT> </DIV>
<DIV><FONT size=3D2 face=3DArial>Yeomans, Donald K.
Near-Earth Objects: =
Finding Them=20
Before They Find Us, Princeton University Press,
2013</FONT></DIV>
<DIV><FONT size=3D2 face=3DArial></FONT> </DIV>
<DIV><FONT size=3D2=20
face=3DArial></FONT> </DIV></DIV></DIV></DIV><
/DIV></DIV></DIV=
></DIV></DIV></DIV></DIV></DIV></DIV></DIV></DIV>
</DIV></DIV></DIV>=
</DIV></DIV></DIV></DIV></DIV></DIV></DIV></DIV></DIV><
/DIV></DIV></DIV><=
/DIV></DIV></DIV></DIV></DIV></DIV></DIV></DIV></DIV></
DIV></DIV></DIV></=
DIV></DIV></DIV></DIV></DIV></DIV></DIV></DIV></DIV></D
IV></DIV></DIV></D=
IV></DIV></DIV></DIV></DIV></DIV></DIV></DIV></DIV></DI
V></DIV></DIV></DI=
V></DIV></DIV></DIV></DIV></DIV></DIV></DIV></DIV></DIV><
/DIV></DIV></DIV=
></DIV></BODY></HTML>

------=_NextPart_000_0008_01D1602E.14DA7BC0--

9 781700 541109